Cover:
www.monaho.com



Photo Contributors:
www.monaho.com
Darrell and Stephanie Arii
Angeline Alba Gueco
Umeko Iseri Konno
Bernice Hahn Yanagawa


Printed in Canada

# *One Cup Rice*

Also by Hazel K. Ho:

*The Salmon Fishing Adventure:*

*How to Locate, Lure and Land*

*the Big Salmon and More . . .*

# *One Cup Rice*

Hazel Kazuko Arii Ho

**A Plus Publishing**
**Honolulu, Hawaii**

# *One Cup Rice*

Published by:

A Plus Publishing
P.O. Box 161237
Honolulu, Hawaii 96816
U.S.A.
www.a-plus-publishing.com

© 2007 by Hazel Kazuko Arii Ho

ISBN-10: 0-9742682-1-6
ISBN-13: 978-0-9742682-1-7

Portions of this book previously appeared in The Salmon Fishing Adventure: How to Locate, Lure and Land the Big Salmon and More…
www.salmonfishingadventure.com

This book is dedicated with love to:

Brothers: Henry Saichi Arii and Harvey Jiro Arii

Sisters: Gladys Setsuko Tomita, Judith Mieko Luke, Mildred Tomiyo Kipu, Violet Suyeko Arakaki and Gertrude Hiromi Nakamura.

Children:  Robert Dale, Rhonda Lynn and Ramona Anne.

Granddaughters:  Brigid Maile and Jessica Jo.

My soul mate:  Robert Kim You Ho

# ACKNOWLEDGMENTS

Thanks to my grandparents who had the courage to leave the comforts of their homes in Japan to pursue a dream of a better life. They took great risks, met challenges, overcame many hardships, and planted strong roots in a strange new world:

> Genjiro Arii and Shige Matsumura,
> Otomatsu Iseri and Toyo Yutaka

Thanks to my parents who struggled and sacrificed. They paved the way with their love, and taught me many life lessons:

> Henry Seiso Arii and Tomeko Iseri

Thanks to my multiracial family—blood relatives, relatives by marriage, and by hanai (adoption)—who empowered me with confidence and courage to weather the many challenges of my life's journey.

Ariis, Matsumuras, Iseris, Yutakas, Uratas, Omoris, Takedas, Inouyes, Abes, Konnos, Wakuzawas, Harukis, Shodas, Tomitas, Kipus, Tokuhisas, Kiyabus, Arakakis, Hamamotos, Misakis, Nakamuras, Shiroishis, Sakamotos, Yanagawas, Uyedas, Hos, Lukes, Suans, Pangs, Lees, Leongs, Wongs, Chongs, Auyongs, Youngs, Herveses,

Graces, Saraons, Rillamases, Estepas, Menors, Goleses, Albas, Guecos, Torreses, Tavareses, Andrewses, Hahns, Harts, McCormacks, Nelligans, and O'Sheas.


Thanks to all the extraordinary people—so many—who befriended and mentored me . . . I am a more fulfilled human being now than when first we met.

# ABOUT THE AUTHOR

Hazel Kazuko Arii Ho, is a third generation (sansei) Japanese-American woman, born the year Captain Charles Lindbergh crossed the Atlantic in his Spirit of St. Louis from New York to Paris, France. Gasoline was only fourteen cents in the Twin Cities.

In Hawaii—The Honolulu Academy of Arts opened on the site of the former residence of Mr. and Mrs. Charles Cooke, the Waikiki War Memorial Natatorium was dedicated to World War I veterans, and the "Malolo," Matson's first luxury cruise ship, arrived in Honolulu 4½ days after leaving San Francisco.

Growing up in Kalihi—a not so affluent neighborhood in Honolulu—had its down side. Everyone was poor.

The neighborhood—Japanese, Chinese, Hawaiian, Filipino, Korean, and Portuguese—provided the author with a multicultural lifestyle. Celebrations—Japanese *Shogatsu* Chinese *Moon Festival*, Filipino *Tinikling*, Hawaiian *Kanikapila*, Korean *Fan Dance*, and Portuguese *Lapinha*— are memories of a rich and colorful childhood.

The up side of this multicultural lifestyle was the ethnic food—*Sushi* and *sashimi*, *jai* and *juk*, *adobo* and *guisantes*, *poke* and *poi*, *kim chee* and *kalbi*, and Portuguese bean soup and *malassadas*.

Like people and nations with their similarities and differences, the ethnic food—Japanese gyoza, Chinese gau gee, Filipino lumpia, Hawaiian laulau, and Korean mandoo—are basically the same. They are wraps. Each, however, offers a distinct aroma and flavor.

The author lives in Hawaii with husband, Robert, children, and grandchildren.

# ABOUT THE BOOK

How many grains in *One Cup Rice*?

"My cup runneth over. . . ."

Each grain of rice represents a person who touched my life in some way—for better or worse. Not any one is, in any way, more or less important than the other. Together they have honed me into the human becoming I am today.

This book is a selection of life stories of the people who are in my *One Cup Rice*. Perhaps, you are one of those people, or you may have some just like them in your cup.

# CONTENTS

Prologue                                           1

Because Mom Said So                                3

Mother                                             7

The Seamstress                                     9

Harmonica Man                                     11

Poor Man's Soup                                   13

*One Cup Rice*                                    15

Math Lessons                                      17

The Doll                                          19

Promises                                          21

My Forever Teacher                                23

Strong Teeth, Strong Carter                       25

Saturday Mornings at the Liliha Theater           26

Down Hill Racer                                   27

Silver Bullets                                    29

Ice Cream, Cake and Harvey                    31

The Settlement                                32

Thanksgiving Chicken                          33

 Busted Pie                                   35

Neighborhood Mom and Pop                      37

Pac-Pacs                                      39

What's In a Name?                             40

Terror In The Night                           41

A Mouse Named Mickey                          43

Jimmy, Come Home                              46

Jay                                           47

A Chilling Summer                             49

Happy Dress                                   51

Lady Luck                                     53

The Red Jacket                                55

Memory Lanes                                  57

Ojiisan:  Grandfather Arii                    61

A Promise Kept                          65

It's Not Your Time                      67

My Two Geishas                          69

Grandpa Iseri's White Horse             77

Quick, Under The Bed                    81

Zero'd                                  85

Nanay:  A Casualty of War               87

The General's Car                       91

My Favorite Aunty                       93

Kalihi Uncle's Friend                   97

Scholarship or Job?                     99

Big Sis, "Lil"                          100

Not Love At First Sight                 101

Sandwich, Anyone?                       103

Honeymoon Cottage                       105

Best Performance of the Year            107

A Girl on Girls' Day                    108

Never Go To Bed Angry    109

Soul Mates    111

The Eyes Have It    113

Christmas, Everyday    115

The Best Daughter-in-Law    117

Call Me, "Popo"    120

Seven Elevens    121

Big Brother    123

Aquarium    125

A Dog's Best Friend    126

The Best Christmas Tree in the World    127

New Year's Eve at Popo's    128

Don't Bring Me Flowers When I'm Dead    129

Goodbye, Patches    131

Return On Investments    135

Smoke-free Facility    137

Young Doctor Brigid    141

Grandpa's Garden                                     143

One Man, Two Hands, Millions of Seed                 144

Lady On The Lake                                     145

Snagged In The Eye                                   147

Cry Tomorrow                                         149

Yurei:  Ghost                                        151

Autumn of My Bald Eagle                              153

A Tale of Two Whales:  A Close Encounter of          157
      The Awesome Kind

Lessons From My Arbor                                159

My Cup Runneth Over                                  163

Epilogue                                             165

Glossary                                             169

# PROLOGUE

*One Cup Rice* is a gift to my family and friends.

The best part of our family potlucks was not the food—it was the "talk story" time. A re-telling of an incident would bring laughter, tears, and most always "that's not the way it happened. . . ." The story sometimes took on a life of its own, depending on who was telling it.

Our children began asking questions. "How did you two—so opposites—ever get together? Was it love at first sight?"

Granddaughters interviewed us for class assignments. "How did you and Grandpa meet? Where were you when the Japanese attacked Pearl Harbor? Oh, Wow. . . ."

I did my best to tell a truthful story—as best as my memory served. But everyone knows memory, like hearing, is selective, and is a blessing of our senior years.

My decision to write *One Cup Rice* . . . because mom said so.

# BECAUSE MOM SAID SO

"Right."

I have been hearing "right" for the past three days—every time I passed the photograph of mom wearing her "only on special occasion" pearls. Oh, Mom, I really miss you. I turn my thoughts to happy times—the best birthday present, the special red jacket, the senior prom gown. The lump in my throat gives way to a flood of tears. Mom's memorial service was only a week ago.

Mom was never a physically strong person, but she was one tough lady, mentally and spiritually. Her frail health, I later understood, was due to her having had one baby after another—eight of us—about two years apart.

Unlike my girlfriends, who occupied their time talking and dreaming about boys, my life was very different. As the eldest child, I spent much of my time after school doing chores. I was busy cleaning house, washing and ironing, buying groceries and cooking meals, bathing my younger siblings, helping them with their homework, and reading or singing them to sleep. This was not the carefree life of a thirteen-year-old.

I could not have done all the housework and child care without mom's patience and encouragement. "It's not that hard . . . I'll teach you how to . . . do it right. Take your time . . . don't rush . . . do it right. Good girl, I knew you could . . . do it right." Her common sense, down-to-earth, loving and caring philosophy was her strength and, later, mine.

The whines, groans, and tears brought on by seemingly impossible situations in my early life were ignored by mom.  Instead, she presented each task, problem, or setback as challenges—"practice," she said—that gave me the strength and stealth of hind's feet later in life.

~◊~

Again, I heard mom say, "right."  What about "right," Mom?  Move your photo to the right?  I did something right?  What?  Mom, what are you trying to tell me?
"Write."
Mom said, "Write!"

Mom:  Mrs. Tomeko Iseri Arii

Young Tomeko Iseri

Tomeko (left) and friend

# MOTHER

You gave me life,

Laughter and sorrow we shared,

You comforted me.


Pearls of wisdom flowed,

Forever memories mine,

I am rich with love.


My journey begins,

Thanks, Okaasan, I love you,

Now it is my time.


Hazel Kazuko Arii Ho

Mom:  You gave me life, love,
and . . . designer dresses

# THE SEAMSTRESS

Mom was a talented seamstress. She could design and sew anything I wanted. All I had to do was show her a picture from a magazine. It was a blessing that she could do this because we could not afford any store-bought clothes.

We were told to have a blue and white dress for class day and a white dress for graduation. We could afford only one dress. Mom designed a blue vest from a piece of remnant that she had saved from another project. I wore the vest over a white dress for class day. I was happy with the same white dress on graduation day at Kawananakoa Intermediate School. My creative mom, she always made me look great.

Ruffles were the "in-thing" this year. We were ready to take pictures for our Farrington High school yearbook. I selected a light blue fabric but wanted full ruffles on the neckline—like a "lei." Mom bought some organza fabric and special-ordered a ruffled collar from the Singer Sewing Machine Company. On picture-taking day, Sally and Jane wore limp, flat ruffles on their blouses. I wore a lei of delicate white butterflies.

~◊~

Two months before my Senior Prom, I scouted stores downtown to look for a prom gown. The gown in the store window at Liberty House we couldn't afford, but I knew mom could sew one just like it.

I began sketching. Mom just stared. "Come on in and try it on," the store clerk offered. We lowered our eyes and mumbled a barely audible, "Just looking . . . thank you."

~◊~

Senior Prom night . . . I was the envy of my girl friends who "oohed and aahed" over my strapless, black satin-trimmed, pink lace gown. Mom added tiny baby rosebuds at the empire bodice—a whole new fashion to my *Iseri* designer gown.

"String of Pearls," "Moonglow," "Dancing in the Dark," "I Could Have Danced All Night. . . ."

# HARMONICA MAN

*Momotaro* (Peachboy), *Issun Boshi* (The One Inch Boy), *Hanasaka Jijii* (The Old Man Who Made Trees Bloom), *Urashima Taro* (The Man Who Visited the People of the Sea)—we never tired of listening to mom read our favorite Japanese folk tales.

When mom was busy with household chores, it was dad's turn to put his three girls, Sets, Mie, and me, to bed. He did not read to us. He played his harmonica. He played many of our requests—"Hato poppo" (The Bird Song), "Yuyake Koyake" (The Evening Song)—Japanese children's songs.

Dad played Hawaiian songs, too—"Aloha Oe, "Maui Chimes." My favorite was "E Meow Meow Oi." "Daddy, play my meow meow cat song for me."

Sister Mie's high meows, sister Sets' low meows, and my long meeeeeows, howled along with dad's harmonica music. We sounded like a bunch of alley cats until somebody started giggling. We rolled on the bed, laughing so hard until we couldn't breathe another meow and there was only shrill wheezing sounds coming from dad's harmonica.

Before we could catch our breath, our scowling, hands-on-hips mom would suddenly appear at the bedroom doorway.

"Daddy, you supposed to be putting them to bed, not play cat games!"

How I loved my meow meow cat song.

"Play it again, Dad!"

Years later I learned that the bedtime song my dad played on his harmonica was not the meow meow cat song. The title of the song: "Imi Au Ia Oi," by Charles E. King.

Harmonica Man

"Soup's on . . . come and get it. . . ."

Dad had cooked his favorite soup and was calling us to dinner.

I could never get over the fishy smell of sardines and would make all kinds of excuses to avoid eating dad's soup.

"Oh . . . uh, I'm going to do my homework now . . . I'll eat . . . maybe, later. . . ."

Today, when Robert pops a can of sardines packed in oil, fills the remaining space in the flat can with Tabasco and soy sauce, and gives each sardine a couple of pokes with his chopsticks to soak up the flavors—the attack on my olfactory overwhelms . . . nausea begins.

"Oh . . . uh, excuse me . . . I think I'll go feed the dogs now. . . ."

# ONE CUP RICE

"Oh, Mom . . . not again. Tell Sets to go this time . . . not me. . . ."

I did not want to go to Aunty Sweet Potato's house. This would be the second time this month I had to walk over to her house—head down, shoulders drooped—to borrow *one cup rice.*

It was the end of the month. Mom was unable to stretch dad's meager earnings as a mechanic, to buy a bag of rice (Rice came in 100-pound bags in those days).

One cup of kome (uncooked rice) cooked to gohan (cooked rice) would not feed a family of eight. But one cup of rice cooked into okai (rice soup) with chunks of sweet potatoes from mom's garden kept eight stomachs quiet through the night.

Aunty Jane, on the heavy side, was always smiling and laughing. Uncle Harry, her husband, was thin and grouchy. They were not rich—just very generous, sharing what little they had with our family. When mom tried to repay with interest—*one cup rice* with two—Aunty Jane would not have it. She insisted she would rather dig up some sweet potatoes from mom's garden; hence her nickname: "Aunty Sweet Potato."

I will always remember the lesson Aunty Sweet Potato taught me. Through her example, I learned about the cup of human kindness and the power of *one cup rice.*

Aunty "Sweet Potato" Jane and granddaughter, Arlene

# MATH LESSONS

Mathematics: My most favorite worst subject. Dad noticed my difficulty with this subject and began helping me with my homework.

Dad was good with his hands. He could fix almost anything.

He fixed my math problems with a deck of cards. I learned to count the spots of clubs, diamonds, hearts, and spades; recognize the numbers on the cards; add, subtract, multiply, and divide—all from one deck of 52 playing cards. Needless to say, I learned to add up to 21 real fast. Beating my dad at Black Jack was fun.

Fraction lessons began after dinner. Dad brought out one apple from the icebox and set it on the kitchen table. He cut the apple in two halves, then one half again into fourths. Dessert? Dad shared more than his apple with me.

"Remember, there are eight of us," Dad said. Cutting the pie into eight pieces was easy.

Fractions were no longer a problem but mathematics remained my most favorite worst subject—unless there was a pie in the equation.

Thanks, Dad. You made learning fun, easy, and delicious.

Math Teacher

# THE DOLL

The doll. We were not allowed to play with her—dress her up, comb her hair, or hug her. We could only gaze at her, protected in her original cellophane-covered display box, as her never blinking eyes looked down on us from the corner shelf she shared with the cathedral radio.

This one doll was a Christmas gift for all three girls—Sets, Mie, and me—because our parents could not afford one for each of us. So we would not fight over it, the rule was none of us could play with her; also, it "cost plenty money." Soon we lost interest in the doll and looked to other things to play with.

I shared my pickup sticks dad made for me. Each chopstick was carefully carved and painted. I treasured this gift he made with his own hands—the same steady hands I could never beat at the game.

Sets kept us laughing with her coconut button-eyed sock puppet mom crafted for her. Sets was good at making up stories.

Mom made bean bags filled with wiliwili seeds for Mie. We played a game much like dodge ball, where players tried to bean each other with a bag.

A player would target another player, aim, and throw a bean bag; hopefully, making a hit, and all the while running around trying not to get hit. The rule was to aim at legs only, but my athletic skills were poor, so I was dangerous.

We had fun sharing and playing with our homemade toys and games—strings, boxes, cans—whatever our imagination could create from these simple, common, around-the-house items. We played with twigs, leaves, seeds, pods, and even mud.

Poor doll, poor pretty Shirley Temple doll—always clean, in her pretty dress, and lonely—nobody to play with.

Years later, Shirley Temple doll mysteriously disappeared. We paid so little attention to her, we didn't even know when she left.

# PROMISES

"Mom, David didn't come to school today, I wonder if he's okay." Mom's eyes told me something was wrong.

Mom cupped my face in her hands and drew me closer to her. She whispered, "Kay . . . (there was a long pause). David . . . (another pause). Kay, I'm so sorry, David died last night."

"What? No, it can't be. I just saw him yesterday . . . we went to pick guavas. . . ." I cried so hard, I couldn't breathe to speak. "Oh, David . . . I promised . . . I wouldn't tell. . . ."

My best buddy, David and I loved the mountains and streams that gave life to "our" trees. Whatever the season, we knew where there was always something for the pickings—mountain apples, avocados, bananas, lychees, papayas, and lots and lots of mangoes.

We could already taste the jam our moms would make with the guavas we picked today.

I shouted up the tree, "David, 'nough already, come down."

David stretched his body along a branch and reached out for just one more.

It happened so fast—the crack of the branch, swoosh and the thud of David's body against a huge boulder hidden just below the surface at the water's edge. His lifeless body did not move, and his eyes did not open. Now hysterical, I cried and screamed his name . . . "David! David . . . ?"

Realizing my fear was real and now feeling a bit guilty, David flashed his rascal smile. He started laughing but at the same time winced from the pain of his fall.

I was so angry at David for scaring me by pretending to be dead, but his contagious laugh infected me and I started laughing, too.

"Kay, please don't tell my mom what happened or I'll be in big trouble. Don't tell your mom, too, or she'll tell my mom. Please, please, don't tell, okay? Promise?"

"Oh, okay, I promise."

Mom held my hands together between hers as though we were praying. She spoke slowly so I would understand. "Kay, when something bad happens to you or to anyone else and it is a matter life or possible death, promise me, 'you will tell'."

# MY FOREVER TEACHER

She read me stories of kings and queens, princes and princesses, fairy godmothers, witches, and goblins—all those wonderful fairy tale people with their "once upon a time and happily ever after."

I began to read for myself.

By fourth grade, I had read all the fairy tale books— *Grimm's Fairy Tales*, *The Golden Fairy Tale Book*. I read books for and about girls—L.M. Montgomery's *Anne of Green Gables*, Louisa May Alcott's *Little Women*.

When I told Mrs. Bains I had read all the girls books, she suggested I read the books for boys. "Who knows, you may enjoy them." I lived life on the Mississippi with Mark Twain and played with Tom Sawyer and Huck Finn. These adventures released a spirit in me that got me into trouble more times than I care to remember.

Mrs. Bains soon realized I was reading the same books over and over. "Kazuko, come here. Look at this book list and choose the books you'd like to read."

"Really? Any book I want?"

"Stop, that's enough. We only have money for a few new books this time. Maybe, we can buy more next month."

It didn't take long for me to finish reading the new books, and I waited anxiously for the next book list.

Mrs. Bains said, "Reading is fine, but listening is important, too." She played a record on the phonograph for me. I read the story of "Aida" by Giuseppe Verdi so I could understand the music. I never heard such beautiful music.

Mrs. Bains took me on a stimulating journey on the history of world art. The art of the Renaissance—the latter half of the15h century, and the 16$^{th}$ century—became my favorite. I remembered Mrs. Bains that day at the Louvre Museum when I smiled back at the "Mona Lisa" and stood in awe of Michelangelo's "David," in Florence..

Many years later, I discovered among my mother's souvenirs, a hollowed out chunk of clay with tiny little thumb prints along the bottom and sides. Like missing teeth, two pieces of clay pinched out from opposite sides of the rim made my objet d'art a functional as well as a decorative piece. Michelangelo Buonarroti, I'm not.

Mrs. Flora Bains, Librarian, Lanakila Elementary School. To her, I owe:

My wonderful imagination, that leads me into realms beyond.

My spirit of adventure—walked and climbed the Great Wall of China, gazed in awe at the snowcapped summit of Mount Fuji, smiled back at the Mona Lisa, basked in the glow the City of Lights from the Eiffel Tower, white water rafted the Colorado River, salmon fished the pristine waters of Alaska, humbled by the mighty sequoias, and more.

The rewards of patience: I have received many life rewards just when I was about to lose my patience.

The fine art of listening—to everything and everyone—whether as a sympathetic listener to my family and friends, enjoying the cardinal singing to its mate from the uppermost branch of my avocado tree, or as an appreciative patron of the performing arts.

The joy of creating, that releases my inner energy and is the catalyst for my writing.,

Thank you, Mrs. Bains, my forever teacher.

# STRONG TEETH, STRONG CARTER

*"This is the way we brush our teeth, brush our teeth, brush our teeth. This is the way we brush our teeth, so early in the morning."* This childhood refrain was taught to my family—children and grandchildren—and used as part of an effective introduction and training for good dental hygiene.

My introduction to good dental hygiene came from the Health Nurse at Lanakila Elementary School who referred me to the Strong Carter Clinic at Palama Settlement. I received a dental checkup, filling of cavities when needed, and a toothbrush and toothpaste—all this for 10 cents. Before leaving from my appointment, the dentist would insist I remove my toothbrush from its wrappings, squeeze a dab of toothpaste on it and she taught me how to brush my teeth properly—all the while I hummed and sang the words in my head, *"This is the way we brush our teeth. . . ."*

The good dental hygiene practices taught to me early in life by the dentist at the Strong Carter Dental Clinic made a lasting impression on mc. The dental fillings lasted nearly a half a century before they needed to be replaced. Today, at age 80, I still have all of my teeth and enjoy eating anything I want.

Good genes may be partly responsible, but I do believe I owe my strong teeth to Strong Carter.

# SATURDAY MORNINGS AT LILIHA THEATER

It's the H-1 Freeway today, but back then there was the Liliha Theater on Liliha Street, next to the Liliha Dress Shop. There was a market—Piggly-Wiggly, I think—on the corner of Liliha and School Streets. The trolley line ended on School Street.

Saturday mornings were special for Sets and me. Because we could not afford ten cents for each of us, we took turns going to the Saturday morning "double bill" movies at the Liliha Theater. We could not miss any one Saturday because Flash Gordon and Buck Rogers were cliffhangers, and we dare not miss a chapter. I would go one Saturday and tell Sets what happened to Flash, and Sets would go the next Saturday and tell me what happened to Buck. Sets was a better story teller—she could really ham it up.

There were other double bill for the boys, but I was not interested in cowboy movies. I got hooked on science fiction, and today, I'm a "Trekkie," a science fiction nut.

We sneaked homemade cookies and puffed rice-cakes into the theater, hid and munched on them, because we did not have the extra five cents to buy goodies from the theater snack shop.

Saturday morning double bill at the Liliha Theater was a big treat for us kids from a poor neighborhood.

Hmmmm . . . maybe, we were not so poor, after all.

# DOWN HILL RACER

I thought I was going to die. Oh, why did I take the dare? How stupid can I be? I'm going to die.

A few minutes earlier, Ed had dared me to ride the inner tube down the steep hill at Lanakila Park. All the girls were laughing and screaming as they sat on their straw mats and slid down the steep hill. It was the last day of school and this was what the girls did. The boys—they took turns riding a big inner tube down the hill. The first one to reach the bottom and stand up was the winner.

I told Ed, "I can do that."

"Nah . . . you're just a girl."

Those words raised my temperature and my nerves. Mom always said that girls could do anything they put their minds to, and I believed her. Today was not only the last day of school at Lanakila Elementary School, it was the last day of sixth grade. In September, I would be going to Kawananakoa Intermediate School. So, it was my last chance to do what I've wanted to do ever since second grade. I decided, "It's now, or never."

So, there I was curled up inside the inner tube and going downhill so fast I couldn't tell which way was up—all the time thinking, "I'm going to die." The drumming of my heartbeat in my ears grew louder and louder with each turn of the inner tube. My head throbbed each time the tube bumped over a high spot. Just as the hot dog I had for lunch was about to make an encore . . . the rolling and bumping stopped.

Dazed, I untangled myself from the inner tube and barely stood up when . . . Yep, here comes Ed. . . .

Wa . . . chout . . . !"

Too late. . . .

Is she . . . dead?" Sally whispered. I opened my eyes
to a circle of wide-eyed, open-mouthed faces. No wonder, I
was a bloody mess—fresh strawberries on both elbows, and
half a bloody nose.

"I won . . . I won!" I shouted as I strutted off.

"Come on . . . two outta three? You was just lucky."

"No, Ed . . . I wasn't just lucky . . . 'I'm just a girl,'
who won."

For many years after that down hill race at Lanakila
Park, the hill didn't look steep at all.

Today, to this 80-year-old senior citizen, that
hill looks just as steep as it was to the then 12-year-old
tomboy.

# SILVER BULLETS

Silver bullets. What's the first thing you think of when someone says, "Silver bullets." Werewolf—how to kill a werewolf—right? Wrong!

These silver bullets were for healing, not killing. They were half the size of BB shots. My BB gun was a hand-me-down from cousin Henry. Practice involved shooting dimes lodged on the wooden fence 20 paces away. Any dime you shot off the fence was yours to keep. That's another story.

Getting back to silver bullets—these were in a small box with Japanese words written on them. This small box contained 12 silver bullets. The box was one of many other various-sized boxes and bags with Japanese writing on them—all in a small drawstring bag. Mom hung this medicine bag on a nail right next to the icebox.

Whenever one of us got sick, mom would go to the medicine bag, read the Japanese words, and give us whatever was in a particular box—red pills, yellow tablets, white powder. I remember the silver bullets.

At the first sign of a cold, especially fever, out came the box with the silver bullets. I always resisted taking the two silver bullets that looked like BB shots. Mom would check my mouth—under my tongue—to make sure I swallowed them.

The silver bullets worked . . . I was off to school the following day.

Life was simple . . . All you needed to do was go to your own in-house pharmacy—the medicine bag. Every month, the Japanese medicine man inventoried, replaced what was missing, and charged a small fee for what was used.

Today, prescription drugs are a very complicated matter with names and ingredients I can't pronounce, and side effects that are worse than what ails you. The high cost of drugs to maintain good health is fast becoming prohibitive. People are faced with difficult decisions . . . food or medicine?

Come back silver bullets . . . come back medicine bag.

Come back good old days.

# ICE CREAM, CAKE, AND HARVEY

Not one moan, not even a whimper. I was old enough to know what was happening. The midwife had arrived and took mom into the bedroom. Of all days, why did she have to have her baby today? It's my birthday!

Earlier, mom had prepared a birthday party for me. Eating sushi, macaroni salad, barbeque beef sticks, and fried chicken, I heard part of a joke, "Did you hear about . . .?"

My thoughts were in the bedroom with mom. Why is it so quiet? I hope she's okay. What's taking so long? It's too quiet, something's wrong. Oh, God, please let mom and the baby be okay.

Cake and ice cream served, friends thanked and gone, I knocked on the bedroom door. As I reached for the doorknob, I heard a weak mewing.

"Come in," Mom said. I placed the tray with the cup of special tea on the bedside table. Mom looked tired, but when she smiled, I knew she was okay.

Mom handed me a wiggling blue bundle.

"Happy Birthday, Kay," Mom said, as she sipped her special tea.

"Thanks, Mom, great birthday present . . . a baby Harvey."

# THE SETTLEMENT

James and Ragna Rath were visionaries. In 1905, they founded the Palama Settlement and Hawaii would never be the same again. They were responsible for saving and enriching many lives through their lifelong commitment to the people of Hawaii.

The "Settlement," was the only place mom allowed me to go to spend my precious free time, only occasionally on Saturdays. Hanging out with friends at Palama Settlement was a treat for me. The Settlement provided the neighborhood kids with recreational and educational activities to keep many of them off the streets and out of trouble. It was a safe haven from abuse by the neighborhood bullies.

In the fourth grade at Lanakila School, I learned to swim at the Palama Settlement pool. As a member of the Farrington High School Girl's Varsity Swim Team, I spent many hours in my small piece of heaven on earth. As my body glided through the water, my mind drifted to far-off places. I learned discipline in every stroke as I pushed the cool water past my body. Through athletic achievement, self-confidence was mine.

A century later, a young New England couple's dream lives on and their legacy continues in the heart of Kalihi.

# THANKSGIVING CHICKEN

I could not bring myself to tell them we couldn't afford a turkey. What kind of Thanksgiving story will they have to share with their classmates when they went back to school?

As an *omimai* (get well gift), Aunty Konno had given mom a chicken—a live one. Our dinner was tied to the clothesline post in the back yard. The problem was I didn't know what to do with a live bird—how to kill it and prepare it. I went to the bedroom to ask mom how I should go about cooking our Thanksgiving chicken.

I tied the chicken's legs with string, locked the wings and pulled off some neck feathers. With my left foot on the squirming chicken, I closed my eyes and made a chopping motion toward the naked neck. Suddenly, I felt warm liquid on my foot, hands, and face. After a quick toe count I dropped the knife and jumped back. Screaming, I hopped, skipped, and jumped, trying to get away from the blood-spurting chicken as it flapped around the backyard.

Lifting the now headless chicken by the legs, I dipped it in the pot of hot water. Pulling off feathers, washing the naked chicken with cold water, salting the whole chicken, inside and out, then rinsing off some of the salt, I was ready to roast the chicken. The rest was easy.

At age thirteen I was able to cook a Thanksgiving dinner for my family—chicken with day-old bread stuffing, gravy from drippings, rice, and vegetables from mom's garden. Sets and I told the chicken story, and younger sisters and brothers laughed as we ate our Thanksgiving dinner. Mom was all smiles as she watched us from her bedroom. Everyone helped clear the table and got ready for our family's favorite—"busted" pie."

Our family truly had much to be thankful for.

# BUSTED PIE

Mom had given birth to our youngest sister, Gertrude Hiromi, the only one to be born in a hospital. I planned to visit mom that evening with her favorite pie.

Dinner and dishes done, I bathed the little ones and started them on their homework. I was exhausted, but within a few minutes I caught my second wind and felt this was a good time for me to bake mom's pie.

Younger sisters and brothers were seated around the table—clapping, poking each other—all eyes on the pie. As I started to bring the pie from the counter to the table, I tripped, clipping the pie plate on the corner of the table. The pie landed, filling side down, on the table. The look on my siblings' faces was the last straw. My knees buckled and the hard wood floor broke my fall. I felt like the pie . . . all busted.

A pair of tiny hands pressed ever so gently upon my shoulders. It was three-year-old Harvey. "Don't cry . . . I like busted pie." Amid tears and laughter, pieces of warm crust and custard filling were spooned into rice bowls. Harvey, bless his soul, was right. We all liked "busted pie."

The Busted Pie Kid

Harvey Jiro Arii

# THE NEIGHBORHOOD MOM AND POP

The mom and pop in this story were the owners of a small grocery store on School Street. Mrs. K. was a heavy-set Japanese woman with dark hair. She spoke in a loud, rough voice. Mr. K.—just the opposite—was thin with salt and pepper hair and soft-spoken.

Mr. and Mrs. K. were good to our family. We could not pay cash every time we went to their store to buy food. Anything we could not grow in our gardens and had to buy—rice, sugar, salt, canned goods, kerosene oil for our stove—was given without question. All we had to do was sign a charge book for the amount of purchase. There were times dad could not pay the bill at the end of the month, Mr. K. said, "No worry, maybe you pay next month." They trusted my parents and treated us with dignity.

"This not library, you know . . ." Mrs. K. would snap when she caught us sitting on the floor next to the magazine stand, reading Superman, Batman, Green Hornet, and Aquaman. My favorite was Wonder Woman. "You going buy, or what . . .?"

Sets and I would buy a nickel bag of crack seed (sticky, juicy, Chinese preserved plums) just to get her off our backs. Mrs. K. always filled the brown bag up to the very top to give us as much as she could. She would then go to the back of the store, leaving us reading comics and eating crack seed. Despite her rough demeanor, Mrs. K. was a softie.

Hanging out at K. Store, reading comic books, and sharing crack seed with my sister Sets, was how I spent my Saturday afternoons at my Library of Comics. The best part of the afternoons was when the last crack seed was gone. We tore the brown paper bag into small pieces and chewed the sticky, tasty juiciness into brown paper wads. We sure got our money's worth.

Happiness is:  Comic books and crack seed.

# PAC-PACS

"Hey, Pac-Pac!" I cringed at the sound of that voice and those hurtful words. I wished the ground would open up and swallow me, or I would miraculously become invisible. The taunting continued mercilessly "Hey, Pac-Pac, where you going? Pac-Pac, Pac-Pac, Pac-Pac. . . ."

Holding back tears of embarrassment and anger, I rounded the corner of the office building and ran to my homeroom, distancing myself from Ed and his ceaseless torment. My nemesis was Ed, yes, the very same Ed who dared me to that death-defying downhill race in an inner tube the last day of sixth grade. The reason he bestowed this awful nickname on me was because of my shoes.

I inherited a pair of black and white Oxfords from my Aunty Hazel. After wearing the hand-me-down shoes for only a couple of weeks, the tops began separating from the soles. In hopes of keeping the only pair of shoes to my name a little longer, I used bobby pins to hold them together. The shoes held but would make a flapping sound with every step I took . . . pac-pac, pac-pac. . . .

Today, my family and friends tease me about having so many pairs I could open a "Size 3 Specialty Shoe Store."

No more Pac-Pacs for me.

# WHAT'S IN A NAME?

A pair of black and white Oxfords was not the only thing I inherited from my Aunty Hazel.

A set of physical education uniform—blouse and bloomers (yes, bloomers)—was given to my mom to be used by whichever of her girls might fit it. So, again, I wore Aunty Hazel's hand-me-down—the blouse (not the bloomers).

Kids in the neighborhood began calling me, "Hazel," and it took me a while before I realized why. "Hazel" was embroidered on the back of my blouse. I let it go. Soon, classmates began calling me "Hazel," and from then on the name stuck.

One day, my friend Sally shared her belief in the meaning of names. Her name, Sally, means light-hearted and fun and we agreed she is that. My name Hazel, means commanding and authoritative . . . "I am not," I protested.

She added, "I read somewhere that people with the letter "Z" in their names are destined to be very successful people."

"If that's true, Sally, I guess I'm going to be twice as successful, my middle name is Kazuko."

Whether I have been a "successful" person, I can't say. However, at the risk of being thought "arrogant," I believe I have succeeded in meeting many of my life's challenges—". . . *Let me count the ways. . . .*"

Mom turned off the bedroom light. She had already reminded me twice, "Go to bed, Kay." This was not the first time I kept reading past my bedtime.

"But, Mom, I only have a few more pages to read." Mom gave me that look . . . "Go to bed or I'll take that book away . . . I mean it."

"Eeeeyah" Something cold grabbed my wrist . . . my book went flying in the air. I hit my head on the half open window—then came the brain freeze. My heart pounded in my ears—I felt faint. My knees wobbled like Jello—I couldn't move. I thought the "thing" was going to tear my hand off. I kept screaming, "Mom, help me, Mom, help." Suddenly the "thing" let go. I fell backwards on my bed.

The hysterical laughter . . . it was mom. The "thing" was mom. I cried and laughed at the same time. Totally focused on the story, I did not hear mom come around the yard to my bedroom window. She caught me hanging halfway out the window reading my book by the light of the full moon and the corner streetlight.

Mom calmed me down with a cup of hot chocolate. "Sorry, Kay . . . didn't mean to scare the moonlight out of you." She handed me the book—covered with dry muddy streaks from having landed in the wet weeds below my window. "Tomorrow," she said, and hugged me, "Goodnight."

The book? Bram Stoker's *Dracula.*

# A MOUSE NAMED MICKEY

"EEEEK. . . ." Sets and I both jumped on the bed the first time we saw him—a ball of dark brown fur with a tan lightning bolt on his rump, black eyes, pink nose and mouth. The ball of fur scurried back into the closet. He was just as startled and frightened as we were. Sets, the brave one, slid off the bed and tiptoed into the closet. I watched from the bed. Moving a shoebox, she discovered a hole in the baseboard. "Ah, hah!" she said, "I know where you live."

Our family could not afford pets—no cat, no dog, no bird, not even a fish—so we decided to keep the hole open to see if the mouse would come back. Sets named the mouse Mickey. Now we had a pet.

Mickey came back the following night. We were ready for him— cookie crumbs on a paper cake plate. As he munched on the cookie crumbs, Sets moved slowly toward Mickey and tried to pet him. Mickey darted back into his hole in the wall. After many attempts to pet him, Sets was able to pat his head, at first, then lift him up in the cup of her hands and stroke him until he decided to jump off to go back to his hole. I, on the other hand, could never touch Mickey—something about his tail gave me the heebie jeebies.

One night, Mickey refused to go back to his hole and was darting about the bedroom. We were so pleased with his playfulness—we were singing and dancing with him. . . .

Mickey: Our First Pet

"What are you kids up to?" We heard mom's voice coming from the living room. Sets rolled up her Wonder Woman comic book and began tapping the floor with it to rush Mickey back to his hole before mom could come into our bedroom. Tap left, tap right, left, right . . . Mickey made two lefts. Then the worst happened, and Sets . . . well . . . tapped Mickey. Mickey lay still on the floor.

After the initial shock of seeing Mickey dead, we both burst into tears. "Oh, Mickey, I'm sorry, I'm sorry" Sets cried. "It was an accident, Sets . . . let's give Mickey a nice funeral. . . ."

We wrapped Mickey in a piece of Hawaiian floral print remnant fabric and placed him in a cut up Cracker Jack box cushioned with toilet paper.

Sets found a rock to pound down the popsicle stick cross on the tiny mound. A bunch of pink cloverleaf flowers, gathered from among the weeds in the backyard, covered Mickey's grave.

We bowed our heads in silence and Sets whispered, "Goodbye, Mickey, I miss you already."

# JIMMY, COME HOME

"Jimmy, come home . . . Jimmy, come home," was the wailing cries of my sister Sets who missed him from the morning he disappeared. Her pleas became less and less as the months passed, but last night she moaned, "Jimmy, come home," in her sleep. I hoped, in time, she would forget.

Dad found a dirty, bony, and sickly dog in the empty lot in Kalihi. The leftover rice and sardine tossed to the dog was quickly wolfed down between growls. The dog followed dad home.

A pink-nosed, white Spitz was discovered under the dirty, brown fur. Soon, Jimmy (Sets named him because she took care of him and trained him) became a playful and obedient family pet.

Jimmy was a fiercely territorial dog who was overly protective of property and family. No one could come into the yard without being acknowledged by one of us, except the Alba children. Jimmy knew their smell and would let them pass through our yard to get to their house.

Our garbage can for kitchen scraps was hung on the Sadoyama side of the fence, because Jimmy would not allow the pig farm man to reach over to our side of the fence.

A dirty, bony, sickly dog barking weakly at the front gate was met with Sets' "Oh, Jimmy, you came home."

Dad finally confessed he had taken Jimmy to Uncle John's farm to be a watchdog.

If Jimmy could talk, bet he could tell us some fabulous stories about his long, three-month journey from the farm in Kaneohe to his home at North School Street.

# JAY

He was hunched over trying to keep the rain from wetting the newspapers under his cheap plastic poncho. My heart went out to him—he looked so small, tired, wet, and cold. I wished I could buy all his newspapers so he could go home, get dry, and warm up with some rice soup. I could not do that—my money was needed for rent, food, utilities, and more. . . .

He entered the door soaked and shivering. In his open palms were a few wet dollar bills, but mostly coins that he had earned. "For the house," he said. I cleared my throat, smiled, and said, "Thank you, Jay, we can use it." I gave him back a quarter.

He loved airplanes and bought a model every time he saved enough money. The finished mobiles hung from the living room ceiling.

Crop-dusting helped pay for his tuition and expenses at Embry Riddle School of Aviation. It was not easy—at times he had to ask for financial help. I didn't mind; especially when he was recuperating from a spinal injury when he crashed one day while crop-dusting. He achieved his life's dream when he received his pilot's license.

Work at the airlines was not easy—starting as a maintenance mechanic. Always working to better maintenance, safety, and services, Jay wrote a maintenance manual for which he was highly commended by the airline industry. He retired as a Vice-President for Aloha Airlines.

Distinguished in Who's Who of the West in the Field of Aeronautics, Jay—my kid brother who always had his head in the clouds—made me proud.

"I want to fly . . ."

Henry "Jay" Saichi Arii

# A CHILLING SUMMER

"I'm so cold . . ." I shivered, "Hon, please get me another blanket. . . ." "I'm . . . still . . . cold . . ." I chattered. I don't understand, August is the warmest month of the year in Hawaii.

Robert placed his old Army blanket over my shaking body and finally decided to lie on top of me. I continued these bouts of cold chills—teeth chattering and body shaking—for three nights. Robert considered taking me to the Emergency Room at Queen's Hospital, but I told him I was not sick—just "so cold."

From 1953-1956, Warrant Officer, Henry Saichi Arii, served with the 521$^{st}$ Engineer Group, 1$^{st}$ Aviation Detachment, stationed at Crissy Field, Presidio of San Francisco. He spent three tours of duty in Alaska—summer through winter—on mapping surveys for Coast and Geodetic Mapping Survey. It was on his second tour of mapping surveys when he and his co-pilot ran into trouble when their helicopter crashed on the tundra.

A few days later, I received a letter from Jay. His helicopter had lost oil pressure, so they were flying low when they crashed near Umiat, a few miles above Kotzbue, Alaska. Stranded with three bars of Hershey's candy bars and one canteen of water, Jay and his co-pilot braved hyperthermia and starvation for three days and three nights.

A civilian helicopter pilot making his last run on his search grid found himself low on gas and was flying low to save gas when he sighted Jay's downed helicopter.

My three nights of cold chills in bed, and Jay's three-night chilling ordeal on the tundra happened on August 21, 22, 23, 1956.

Henry Saichi Arii, en route to
Army Aviation Flight School

# HAPPY DRESS

Sister Vie, is the only daughter, among mom's six girls, who took an interest in sewing and pursued her designer talents. She, like mom, could design and sew anything.

Vie entered and won first prize in the Singer Sewing Machine Dress Design Competition. The first prize-winning dress was made of an ecru-colored, silk brocade fabric with satin trimming. It was the most beautiful dress I had ever seen. I admired it from the first time I saw it, when Vie brought it home from San Francisco. Vie packed it in a dress box and forgot about it.

I needed a cocktail dress to attend a reception and did not have the money to buy a new dress. I remembered Vie's dress and asked if I could borrow it for the night. Vie said she would not let me borrow it, but she would give it to me. I couldn't believe my ears. She said she was happy to see the dress finally being used instead of sitting in a box.

That silk brocade dress saw many special occasions—dressed up with accessories for dinners and dressed down for luncheons. Each time I wore the dress, I would give Vie a report of all the compliments that were paid to my beautiful dress.

Vie was happy, I was happy, and I think the dress was happy, too. What . . . the dress was happy, too?

Well . . . the dress, as the years passed, took on a glow—from ecru, to cream, to a rich golden yellow—Yes, it glowed!

Princess "Vie"

Violet "Vie" Suyeko Arii Arakaki

# LADY LUCK

Stan and I went up to our room at about three in the morning, exhausted. While undressing for bed, I felt something telling me to go back downstairs. This feeling nagged at me as I continued to get ready for bed. "Go downstairs, go downstairs." I decided to listen to the voice. I got dressed, and told Stan I was going back down to the casino. With one lifted eyebrow and the other eye already asleep, Stan mumbled, "'kay."

I sat down at my sister Sets' favorite Keno machine. We used to sit side-by-side, rhythmically feeding quarters to these insatiable monsters. Sometimes the machine was nice to us and gave us back some of our quarters. Mostly, though, it kept its feeding frenzy.

I dozed off for a moment when the loud ringing of bells startled me. "Somebody hit something big," I murmured. The bells kept up their deafening noise. "Somebody hit something big, really big . . . 'nough already. Somebody, turn off the noise . . . . "

What I thought was noise only moments ago turned out to be sweet music to my ears. "Oh, wow, it's me . . . it's my machine . . . I hit something . . . the big one?" While waiting for the attendant to come and pay my jackpot, I felt the presence of my sister Sets. I was happy to know that she was still looking out for me.

"You were always my 'Lady Luck' Sets . . . thanks."

My sister, Mil, told me this story while she sat at Sets' lucky Keno machine, waiting for the attendant to come and pay her jackpot . . . again.

"Mil"

Mildred "Mil" Tomiyo Arii Kipu

# THE RED JACKET

It was my first summer working in the Dole Pineapple Cannery.  I lied about my age, so I could work with my friends, a year older than myself, and get to meet cute boys.  More importantly, the family needed my 60 cents per hour pay.  As a trimmer, my thumb soon turned black and blue from holding up the large pineapple and twirling it around to trim both ends.  Also, I developed a rash on my wrists and forearms that began itching and bleeding.  The forelady took pity on me and reassigned me to the packing side of the conveyer belt.  I survived three summers.

My first paycheck, handed over to my mom, was tagged to help pay for rent and other living expenses.  I had been eyeing a red hooded rain jacket in the window of the Liliha Dress Shop for weeks.  I wished I could have it to keep the cold wind and rain off me when I walked to work in the mornings.  Everyday I passed the store, "Oh, good, it's still there."  Then one day, "Oh, no, it's gone."  Oh, well, I knew in my heart that I was hoping for too much.  There were more pressing needs for our family.

My sisters and brothers were fed, bathed, and tucked in for the night.  Mom handed me a box wrapped in red crepe paper and tied with a ribbon of red yarn.  I couldn't believe I was getting such a pretty gift.  It wasn't my birthday.  I wondered what it could be.

"Just open the package," Mom smiled.

A blur of red . . . "My red jacket!"

My resourceful mom, she had a will and found a way—layaway.

# MEMORY LANES

**Pua Lane:** Pua Lane is a short lane beginning at Vineyard Street and ending on King Street. Grandpa Arii lived in Pua Lane in a large two-story frame house. The whole family gathered there for Sunday dinners. These Sunday dinners were held at the insistence of Grandpa who believed that this was the best way to keep family together. No weak excuses . . . anyone who couldn't make Sunday dinner had better have a darn good reason, like giving birth to twins.

Years later, I learned from a classmate at one of my high school reunions, our Arii family Sunday dinners were viewed by some neighborhood kids as that rich family having a "party" every Sunday.

The "parties" were simple dinners with aunts, uncles, and cousins cleaning, preparing, and cooking mostly seafood caught by torch fishing the night before. Strips of white eel soaked in teriyaki sauce cooked over charcoal were pupus enjoyed with cold beer. Small fish boiled and strained into stock made delicious *miso* soup. *Kumu niitsuke* topped a bed of *somen*. *Tako* was boiled in beer and served with *miso* sauce. Sweet slipper lobsters with drawn butter, and vegetables from mom's garden—all part of a regular Sunday family dinner.

**Robello Lane:** Robello Lane begins on King Street and ends on Dillingham Boulevard. My friend, Bea, lived in Robello Lane. She lived in a most unusual house—one with a small, swinging trap door in the back wall of her brother's bedroom. This door reminded me of a doggie door in the kitchen that allows a dog the freedom to come and go as he pleases. Bea, my sister Mil, and I used this door many times when we sneaked out of Bea's house to go swimming at San Souci beach.

Shirabe's Saimin stand in Robello Lane served the best saimin in all of Palama. When the lunch whistle blew at the Dole Pineapple Cannery, Jane and I would run through the cannery, sometimes forgetting to take off our cap and apron. Mrs. Shirabe, knowing we had only 30 minutes for lunch, had our saimin ready for us. We never tired of her saimin—we slurped it down, almost daily, all summer.

**Desha Lane:** Desha Lane starts from Vineyard Boulevard and ends on King Street. Stories whispered among kids in the neighborhood told of Desha Lane being haunted by a ghost. The ghost was a lady in white who floats down the lane on dark, moonless nights, wailing for her lost child. There are variations of this urban legend. I never walked through Desha Lane—not even during the day. Scared? You bet!

Pua Lane, Robello Lane, and Desha Lane are still there in the Palama district.

Today, whenever I drive by these special memory lanes . . . I hear Grandpa's deep, from his gut laughter, I smell the aroma of Mrs. Shirabe's saimin *dashi,* and I feel the hairs on my arms and the back of my neck stand up just thinking about the lady in white.

The Arii Family, circa 1935

# OJIISAN: GRANDFATHER ARII

Genjiro Arii, the firstborn and only son of the Arii family, emigrated from Yamaguchi Ken, a province on the island of Honshu, Japan. At age 26 he left Japan to seek his fortune in a strange new world. As a steerage passenger, he departed the port of Yokohama on the immigrant ship, Miike Maru, arriving in Honolulu on May 29, 1891.

After completing his 3-year contract as a laborer and later as a "luna," foreman, in the sugar cane fields on the island of Hawaii, Ojiisan (Grandfather) moved his family to Oahu. He worked as a peddler, and later as a cooper—one who makes or repairs barrels or casks—for Matson Navigation Company. With his own special homemade noodles, he opened two saimin shops—the first on King Street and the second on Sheridan Street. His okazuya (delicatessen) and, later, a restaurant on Sheridan Street, were said to have served the best sushi in Pawaa. Ojiisan was an entrepreneur and a successful restaurateur.

I was "spoiled" by Ojiisan—kimonos, obis, *kanzashis* (hair ornaments), parasols, slippers, jewelry—he showered me with gifts. Tuition for odori (dance), shamisen and koto (music), ikebana (flower arrangement), chanoyu (tea ceremony) and saiho (sewing)—classes of Japanese culture and refinement expected of a proper, and well-bred Japanese girl—was paid for by Ojiisan.

Ojiisan made sure I was just as tough as the boys—he taught me how to fish. Starting with a simple bamboo pole, using small balls of fresh white bread for bait, he took me to the ocean and taught me patience. It was never only about the fish or fishing. Later, he left me on a skiff, playing with a baby octopus (I loved the crackling, popping sounds when I peeled the tentacles off my arms), while the men walked the reefs—torching (night fishing). I learned to satisfy my curiosity about sea creatures and not be afraid . . . of the dark.

I was fortunate to have Ojiisan help me with my Japanese Language School homework. He was especially knowledgeable about the history of Japan. He told me I was born in *Showa ninen* (the second year of the Showa Era). He was especially proud of the fact that he had chosen my Japanese name, Kazuko. The kanji (Chinese character used in Japanese writing) for my name "Heiwa," means "Peace." Translated, my name, Kazuko, means Child of Peace.

Ojiisan believed in education—not just for the boys—for girls, too. His kind of thinking was rare for a Japanese man of his generation. I later learned how much he believed in an education for me. At graduation from Farrington High School, my concerns about tuition for college were allayed when dad told me Ojiisan had set aside an educational trust fund for me.

At age 75, Ojiisan was hospitalized for chronic common duct obstruction due to gallstones. Four days after surgery, he was readmitted for reconstruction of the common duct. The doctors did not know why his surgical site would not heal.

For two weeks, I walked after school from Hongwanji Japanese Language School to Queen's Hospital to feed him dinner, give him water, cover him with an extra blanket, fluff up his pillows. . . . I did my Japanese school homework in his hospital room. I was the only one with him when, between his rasping, labored breathing, he murmured, "*Kazuko, nakuna . . . itsu made mo . . .*" (*Kazuko,* don't cry . . . forever). I knew he would always be with me and I was comforted.

Time stopped. . . . The mewing stopped. . . .

I lifted my tear-stained face from Ojiisan's chest.

I pressed the call button for the nurse. . . .

Ojiisan (Grandfather):  Genjiro Arii

# A PROMISE KEPT

Grandpa Arii and I were very close. Grandpa spoiled me. Those times when mom and dad denied me things because they could not afford them, or I was not ready for them, all I had to do was run across School Street to Grandpa's house and he would buy whatever I wanted.

"Your last promise and you didn't keep it. Instead, you went and died!"
Sitting in front of Grandpa's grave—the only marker made of red marble in the Moiliili Cemetery—I was feeling sorry for myself. "Why? You always kept your promises. Why not this last one?"

"Hey, anybody home? Look what I got for you, Kay . . . I don't know why . . . I just thought you might like one, so I stopped by Sears. . . ." Breaking open the box and tossing out the packing material . . . yes, there it was . . . a brand new Royal portable typewriter. I thanked dad for buying the typewriter, but I knew I had to thank one more person.

I knelt and placed yellow button chrysanthemums, his favorite, in the vase. "Thank you, *Ojiisan*. Please forgive me for doubting you yesterday. You always keep your promise."

Grandpa Arii's Grave
(Left to right)
Richard, James, Henry (dad), and Harry
(Missing from photo: Pete)

# IT'S NOT YOUR TIME

The sound of the wooden clappers announced the ending of yet another live Japanese theater play—one of many Grandpa Arii and I enjoyed. The curtains were being drawn on the main stage and the last of the characters was scurrying along the *hanamichi* (the passageway that runs from the rear of the theater to the center stage).

People began to leave. I stood up and held on to Grandpa's hand, ready to leave with him. He turned around and smiled.

"You can't come with me. You must go on by yourself. Don't be afraid, I'll always be with you."

"Please, don't leave me, I want to go with you."

"It's not your time. . . ."

My recurring dream stayed with me for many years after the death of my Grandfather. I was his first granddaughter and I always knew I was "special" to him. The bond between us seemed to go beyond. . . .

Many times in my life, my "whys?" have been answered by Grandpa's "It's not your time. . . ." I am comforted by my belief that when it is "my time," Grandpa will, as always, be there for me.

# MY TWO GEISHAS

"Hayaku, hayaku (Hurry, hurry). . . ."

Grandma Arii—a petite, soft-spoken woman—became a General barking out orders when it neared time to ready Aunty Betty and Aunty Hazel for their evening ozashiki (tea house banquet). A whirlwind of activity, grandma pulled out drawers from the tansu (Japanese chest of drawers), taking out under-garments, kimonos, obis (sash), and tabis (socks), and laying them on the bed. Cousin Clara and I set up the mirrored dresser with makeup, hairbrushes, combs, and kanzashi (hair ornaments). The kago (handbag) was readied with maiohgi (dancing fans), hand towel, wooden combs, lipstick—everything needed to complete the geisha (artist of Japanese entertainment) attire.

I was fascinated with the okesho (makeup) part of getting my aunties ready for their evening engagements. A cold, white liquid powder base was plastered on face and neck—they looked like ghosts. Eyebrows were drawn in black, pink powder on cheeks and eyelids, and two dabs of bright red lipstick on upper lip and one dab on lower lip (like a red, baby rosebud) completed their extreme makeup.

Grandma completed the hairdos and dressed my aunties in kimonos and obis appropriate for the season, the status of the client, and the purpose of the banquet.

I do not know when, where, and from whom Aunty Betty and Aunty Hazel received their professional geisha training. Their disciplined training was said to be much like that of a concert violinist, a prima ballerina, or that of any classical Western entertainer. They attained their professional geisha status when they were awarded their geisha names. Aunty Betty's professional geisha name was Hidetaro and Aunty Hazel's geisha name was Emitaro.

Hidetaro excelled at playing the shamisen (a three-stringed instrument with a long neck, square body and played with a plectrum). She was so adept at playing the shamisen she could play not only Japanese songs, but Hawaiian songs and—would you believe—"The Stars and Stripe Forever." Hidetaro accompanied Emitaro who excelled in odori. They were a hard pair to beat.

On days when I stopped by to clean my aunties' rooms, they would be studying. They researched their client—educator, writer, politician, singer, actor—before the evening's engagement so they would be well-informed, knowledgeable and conversant about the client's accomplishments and interests. They were artists of Japanese entertainment and practiced the many disciplines of Japanese culture—art, music, literature, ikebana (flower arrangement), chanoyu (tea ceremony), brush painting, calligraphy. . . .

Their geisha incomes were supplemented with classes for young maiko hopefuls. Japanese mothers begged to enroll their young daughters (six- and seven-year-olds) for Saturday morning odori lessons. Shamisen lessons were held on Saturday afternoons for pre-teens and teenagers.

Cousin Clara and I were reluctant participants in the Saturday morning dance, and afternoon music classes. Before our classes, cousin Clara and I had to dust, wipe, sweep, and mop both aunties' rooms and clean their bathrooms. When I questioned my training as a maid, three whacks on my knuckles with a bamboo saiho ruler was my answer from Aunty Hazel.

"It's part of our training. You know, respect . . .
discipline . . . stuff like that. . . ."

"Gee, Clara, now you tell me. . . ."

Both aunts offered me the opportunity to explore and
appreciate the Japanese performing arts—odori and
shamisen. They soon realized I had problems.

I could not flip a maioghi above my head and catch it
in a graceful dance movement. Try flipping two fans . . .
forget it.

I could not coordinate the finger movement of my left
hand on the three strings at the neck of the shamisen, while
picking the strings on the body of the instrument with a
plectrum in my right hand. The cacophony was not music to
my aunts' ears.

I purposely sang off key and mumbled the lyrics.
Both my aunts gave up on me.

"It's okay . . . I don't care. . . . Anyway, I rather be
fishing with grandpa. . . ."

Hidetaro and Emitaro were so much in demand, they
would entertain at several ozashiki at several tea houses
(Kanraku, Mochizuki, Natsunoya) during the course of a
single evening. They would spend about an hour at one
banquet before departing for another commitment. They
entertained at wedding receptions, anniversaries, special
birthday parties, business parties, and family get-togethers.

Income from their geisha professions, together with
tuition monies from their training classes for young hopefuls,
provided Hidetaro and Emitaro with a rich and independent
life-style—a rare accomplishment for Japanese women of
their generation.

The more enlightened among us know the popular myth that a geisha performs sexual favors is ludicrous. However, as with any profession, there may have been some in the geisha sisterhood whose practice may not have been strictly professional. Hidetaro and Emitaro, however, were from an affluent family, and with their financially independent lifestyle, they had the freedom to practice their art of Japanese entertainment with professionalism.

I believe my two geisha, Hidetaro and Emitaro, were the most beautiful, talented, and classy Japanese ladies of their time. From the many stories shared by geisha sisters, and clients, I learned they were loved and admired by men, women, and children.

Aunty Betty Misao "Hidetaro" Arii

Hidetaro

Emitaro

Young Student

~75~

# GRANDPA ISERI'S WHITE HORSE

He found himself standing waist deep in the dark waters, with no indication of which way was land. Engrossed in his torching, he had lost track of time and place. There were no lights on shore at this isolated fishing spot at Kahana Bay. The only light he had was the small circle of light from his kerosene torch on his back. Dark clouds obscured the stars. Looking down, he saw only still waters with no sound of waves lapping toward shore. Spooky.... Weird....

He took several steps forward and found himself deeper in the water. Was the tide coming up? Afraid to take another step that could plunge him into a hole in the reef, or worse, the channel, he stood frozen, praying for some sign to help him back to shore.

Suddenly, he heard the sound of galloping hooves. He told himself, "Follow the sound, follow the sound. . . . Galloping hooves means a horse . . . a horse means land. . . ." Soon he could make out the outline of a white specter. As he got closer to land, he saw a horse—a white horse—galloping back and forth along the shoreline.

Exhausted, he fell to his knees. Spear and net were dropped. Untying the torch from his back, he extinguished the flame in the sand. When he looked up to thank the horse, there was no horse. He felt a warm breeze brush his face and he knew . . . it was his "luna" white horse that saved him that strange and eerie night at Kahana Bay. Grandpa Iseri breathed a silent "Arigato" (Thank you).

~◊~

Otomatsu, the second son of the Iseri family, emigrated from Kumamoto Ken, a province in Kyushu Island, Japan. At age 24, he left his family in Japan to seek his destiny in a strange, new world. As a steerage passenger of among 1,099 passengers, he departed the port of Yokohama, Japan, on the immigrant ship, the Yamashiro Maru, arriving in Honolulu on June 18, 1891.

Grandpa Iseri's 3-year contract as a sugar cane field worker kept being extended because of debts incurred by a series of misfortunes. The death of his wife, Toyo Yutaka, left him a single parent raising four daughters: Matsue, Sadame, Tomeko and Umeko, the youngest who was a weak and sickly child. Decades later, from January 1913 to May 28, 1916, Grandpa Iseri worked on the Waiahole Water Tunnel Project. This project, more recently identified as the Waiahole Ditch/Tunnel, moves water from Waiahole on the windward side, under the Koolau Range, to Waiawa.

I remember a photograph of Grandpa Iseri riding a white horse. He was a magnificent sight. A tall man, tanned and heavy-set, he looked more Hawaiian, than Japanese. He was promoted from field worker to "Luna," because of his large stature and because he was a good talker—speaking up for the field workers and negotiating terms between the field workers and the "big bosses." The white horse was part of his promotion. The photograph of Grandpa Iseri on his white horse was mounted in an oval frame. Many inquiries of Mom, Aunty Takeda and Aunty Konno failed to produce the whereabouts of this precious memento.

Mrs. Umeko Konno, "Kalihi Aunty" found this photo of her father in an old shoebox. The only dark-complexioned of his four daughters, Umeko looks most like Grandpa Iseri. She was also his favorite daughter, according to my mom when she talked about their "small kid" times.

On the Iseri side of the family I was, again, the first granddaughter and Grandpa Iseri spoiled me. He would turn his pockets out and give me whatever loose change there was—"You go buy rock candy . . . boiled peanuts, okay? Anything you like eat, go buy."

Grandpa Otomatsu Iseri

The Iseris
Matsue, Tomeko (Mom), Grandpa, Umeko, Sadame

Four Sisters: Front: Sadame (center),
Back: Umeko, Matsue, Tomeko (Mom)

# QUICK, UNDER THE BED

"Yay, I got another one. . . ."

"Not . . . I got yours. . . ."

My sister Sets and I were enjoying the aerial show in the sky above the rooftops in the direction of Pearl Harbor. The loud "boom, booms," the dark puffs of smoke, and planes streaking down below the rooflines beyond our view, gave us a movie scenario we were both enjoying.

"Quick, under the bed!" yelled Mom as she came rushing into the house, and pulling us away from the window. I protested, "Why? It's dark and dusty under the bed." Mom quickly pushed us under the bed. "Stay there!"

Early that morning, mom and dad went to the Moiliili Cemetery to visit Grandpa Arii's grave. They rushed home when they realized the sounds of explosions and dark smoke were not our planes practicing. They saw other planes that looked different from ours.

Life began to change. . . .

During the days that followed our radio was always on and we listened to the rules and regulations of Martial Law. We could not play out on the street after dinner because of the 6 PM to 6 AM curfew.

To abide by the rules of the blackout, our windows were painted over with black paint so no lights were visible from the outside. One night there was a heavy pounding on the door. When dad opened the door there were two tall, heavy-set, military policemen looming at the door.

"Yes . . ." dad answered. "What can I do for you?"

"There's a light leaking from one of your windows," growled the MPs who towered over my small Japanese dad. "Better cover it up."

Mom quickly dabbed black paint on the corner of the offending window.

"That's better." Two shadows faded into the dark.

We were so relieved . . . we were not going to be arrested for breaking the blackout law.

Japanese language schools and temples were closed. Teachers who taught at Palama Gakuen were no longer around. I began to miss classmates and their parents, neighbors, and friends. Some people we knew no longer lived in their homes. Where have all the people gone? I learned much later about the relocation camps.

Certain food items were rationed and permits were required for liquor, cigarettes and gasoline. Resourceful Mom—no one in the family drank alcohol, smoked cigarettes and we did not have a car—she exchanged whiskey, Camels and gasoline for canned meats, canned fruits, and vegetables.

Citizens, including children, were issued gas masks that we had to carry with us wherever we went. The principal of Kawananakoa Intermediate School sent me home one day to get my gas mask—the gas mask that didn't even fit my face.

It took the whole family two weeks to dig a hole that was to be our "Bomb Shelter" in the front yard. With the first big rain, this hole in the ground—roofed with old beams and corrugated iron panels—filled with water, caved in, and turned into a muddy pond.

From 1942-1943 public schools were closed one day a week so students could work in the sugar cane or pineapple fields. Clothed in a long-sleeved shirt, pants, a large hat, and covered shoes, I chose to work in the pineapple fields because I loved pineapples. The only thing I didn't like about the work was riding home on the bus and everybody on the bus looking at me suspiciously because I reeked of pineapple sweat.

On Saturdays, I volunteered for the Red Cross rolling bandages. I learned to knit—backs, left fronts, right fronts and sleeves—but I never completed a sweater. Sister Sets had the green thumb so she did the Victory Garden.

Life continued to change. . . .

# ZERO'D

Uncle Takeda was an uncle on my mom's side of the family. He was married to mom's older sister, Sadame. A carpenter by trade, he not only built homes but he created fine cabinets and furniture. The scent of cedar brings back memories of the chest of drawers Uncle Takeda made for mom. This cedar chest had six drawers—one for each of the six girls. I was the top drawer because I was the eldest. When I got married and left home, Sets moved up to the top drawer and each of the younger sisters moved up one drawer.

Uncles and aunties took on names of endearment based on where they lived—Wahiawa Uncle and Aunty, and Kalihi Uncle and Aunty. We lived on School Street so my cousins called my dad and mom School Street Uncle and Aunty.

Just as he did every Sunday, Wahiawa Uncle was on his way to the bakery to buy doughnuts. Wahiawa town is near two military bases—Wheeler Field and Schofield Barracks. Wahiawa Uncle saw and heard more than the usual number of planes that Sunday morning.

Loud explosions and black smoke alerted Wahiawa Uncle that this was not the regular Sunday morning practice. Forgetting the doughnuts, he hurried toward home, just in time to see a plane with the rising sun insignia hurtling down in the distance.

A clap of thunder, a ball of fire, and clouds of black smoke—Wahiawa Uncle knew that it was his house that went up in smoke.  Luckily, the family was not home that fateful Sunday morning when a Japanese Zero fighter plane "zero'd" his two-story home.

Wahiawa Uncle talked about his "*Day of Infamy*" with much sadness—not so much for the loss of his home—for the many lives that were lost at Pearl Harbor on December 7, 1941.

# NANAY: A CASUALTY OF WAR

"Nanay,"—she was the only grandma I knew and loved. Grandma Iseri died when Aunty Konno was three years old, so I never knew her. Grandma Arii never liked me. . . . It was evident in her cruel words and mean treatment of me. I suspect this was because I was Grandpa Arii's first granddaughter and she resented the attention and gifts he showered on me.

Nanay, my Filipino grandmother, always made sure I had lots of Filipino food to eat. My favorite was her delicious chicken adobo. Nanay lived in an old two-story house in Holokahana Lane, in the back of our old house on School Street.

One of our special times together was wash hair day, every Sunday afternoon. After Nanay finished shampooing, I would brush her down-to-her-buttocks black hair. Carefully parting her hair in sections, I applied small drops of her secret coconut oil tonic and gently massaged her scalp. Sunday afternoons with my Nanay were our special talk story time. Her wisdom flowed with each stroke of the hair brush—"Kazuko, you nice girl, take care family, no make shame. . . . " Nanay always encouraged me, "You go school, study hard, you do good, okay?"

"Kazuko, your boyfriend calling . . ." Nanay would announce to the neighborhood.

"Not boyfriend, Nanay, just friend. . . ."

"I don' no, sound like boy to me. . . ."

It was Nanay's generosity in sharing her telephone that kept my social life going during my high school years.

Nanay thoroughly enjoyed watching my dating shenanigans. Early, I would meet my first date on the School Street side of the house. Later, rushing to the back of the house on the Holokahana Lane side, I would meet my second date. Nanay giggled and laughed, all the while vicariously enjoying the goings-on. Still, she said, "Kazuko, you watch out . . . no need boyfriend, just friend . . . no can go college if you get baby."

Then one day . . . "Japanese and Filipinos enemies, now," Nanay said, "no mo' wash hair day, no mo' talk story time, no come my house. . . ."

"But Nanay, you my grandma . . . I love you. . . ."

"No, Kazuko, you Japanese . . . me Filipino. . . . We enemies now . . . no mo' Nanay. . . ."

No amount of reasoning or pleading would move Nanay from her belief that "we enemies now. . . ."

I cried. . . .

I lost my Nanay, the only grandma I knew and loved on Sunday, December 7, 1941.

My Nanay
Maria Goles Alba

# THE GENERAL'S CAR

One of our family's treasures is a memento from World War II. It is a photograph of T/4 Robert Kim You Ho kneeling beside a military staff car with a license plate displaying five stars.

Robert's three-year employment at Navy Yard, Pearl Harbor, Oahu, Territory of Hawaii, qualified him as a Mechanic, First Class. When he was inducted into the Army, he was assigned to the 29th Transportation Corps Car Company at Fort Shafter. His Military Occupational Specialty was Auto Mechanic.

"Yo, Ho," Master Sergeant Jones yelled. "See that car over there? I want you to take special care of that one—maintenance check, tune up . . . the whole works."

When told that their dad drove the General's car during the war, the children were so impressed. They thought their dad was the General's driver. We had to clarify "driving the General's car," to mean a test drive.

Which General?

General Dwight D. Eisenhower.

T/4 Robert Kim You Ho
Military Occupational Specialty (MOS)
Auto Mechanic (014)
29th Transportation Corps Car Company
Fort Shafter, Hawaii
and
General Dwight D. Eisenhower's Staff Car

# MY FAVORITE AUNTY

I was always happy on the first day of school. Every year, from first grade to sixth grade, Kalihi Aunty Konno came to our house with a brown bag containing one composition book, one spelling notepad, one box of crayons and two #2 pencils. "Kay, you the smart one . . . you study hard . . . be doctor. . . ."

"Do you have to get married?" Aunty hesitated. . . .

"No, Aunty, I don't have to get married. . . ."

"Okay, then, I'll pay for your college tuition if you go back to school."

"Thank you, Aunty, but I've decided to get married. Robert said he would pay for my college when I decide to go back."

Kalihi Aunty knew the value of education and was willing to work at two jobs—at the pineapple cannery and an egg company—in order to send me to college. She wanted a life for me that was not possible for her.

Now it was my turn to make Kalihi Aunty happy. On her 90th birthday my sisters, Mil and Vi, and I took her to Las Vegas. I gave Aunty a roll of quarters to play her favorite game—Keno. She lost the whole roll. Mil gave Aunty a roll of quarters—she hit a jackpot! Like most gamblers, Kalihi Aunty is superstitious. She believes that Mil is her "Lady Luck" and insists that she wins only when Mil is present.

Kalihi Aunty Konno—My Favorite Aunty

Mrs. Umeko and Mr. Seijiro Konno
Kalihi Aunty and Kalihi Uncle

# KALIHI UNCLE'S FRIEND

Kalihi Uncle and Aunty, and Mom decided to go fishing on the leeward side of the island. As usual, they ended up at their secret fishing spot in Nanakuli. The shrimp-baited hook, weighted with a split BB shot sinker, was lowered into the moi hole. Mom lit a cigarette and waited. Aunty held her bamboo pole between her knees, and began reading her Japanese magazine. Uncle decided he would try his luck for bigger fish at the next cove.

Uncle was swapping fish stories with another fisherman. The spread of his hands told he was telling another one of his big fish stories.

"Who was that man you were talking stories with?" Kalihi Aunty asked.

"What man?" Uncle looked puzzled.

Without another word, all fishing lines were pulled up, tackle boxes packed, and they raced back to the car.

Agreeing they needed to warm up before their long drive home, they stopped at a coffee shop. A sleepy-eyed waitress brought four glasses of water to the table.

"Why did you bring four glasses of water when there are only three of us?" Mom asked.

"There was four of you guys when you all sat down. . . ."

Mom reached for the shaker—all three fishermen took turns tossing salt over their shoulders.

Kalihi Uncle—Ulua Fisherman

# SCHOLARSHIP OR JOB

Mr. Walton Gordon, principal, Farrington High School, said he would scout around for a scholarship for me to attend the University of Hawaii.

Now, one semester later, the money Grandpa Arii set aside for tuition and books was no longer available because of a financial setback in the family. I needed to support my family—I needed a job.

Mr. Gordon referred me to the Chief of the Accounting Department at Hawaiian Airlines. Work at Hawaiian Airlines lasted only three months. The girls in the office spared no words or actions to let me know that I had usurped the position from more senior employees who felt they were in line for the promotion. I was young, naïve, and I could not handle the shunning. I also agreed that the position should have gone to someone who had worked for and earned it.

Scrubbing ring-around-the-bathtub in the nurses' quarters for the Nursing Supervisor at Leahi Hospital was not my idea of a secretarial position. I politely expressed my objection . . . and left.

"This is absolutely the last time I'm referring you to a job interview," Mr. Gordon threatened. "You'll have to make it work this time, or you're on you own."

The 147th General Hospital across from Fort Shafter, later, Tripler Army Medical Center, became my home away from home for the next 36 years, 3 months, and 10 days.

"You're sitting in my chair . . . and that's my desk," she snapped.

I jumped out of her chair and stood next to her desk.

"Sorry, I was told to sit in that chair and wait for Lillian."

"I'm Lillian. . . ."

Lt. Meserve, Personnel Officer, came from his office.

"Hey, Lil, this is Hazel, your new help."

In the following weeks, Lil introduced me to the girls and GIs in Personnel and to people in the other departments of the 147th General Hospital. She was my mentor—training me in officer payroll, arranging for my Civil Service exams, and helping me to apply for higher GS positions. She treated me to lunch when I attained my "permanent" status.

When Lil learned I was struggling to make ends meet as the sole wage earner for my family, she found me a part-time job as a waitress at the Waikiki Beachwalk Diner. Here again, she worked with me, "to keep an eye on you."

Lil was also a big sister, somewhat over-protective.

"Do you think you can live with him in a small coal mining town in Pennsylvania?"

"Well, he did say he was going back to be the town's orthopedic surgeon."

On another occasion . . . "He's from Alabama . . . how do you think you, a Japanese wife, will survive in the South?"

Lil—my mentor, my friend, my big sister—little did I know at that time, how much more she would become to me.

# NOT LOVE AT FIRST SIGHT

A maroon and white striped hospital robe draped loosely over his bony shoulders, he looked like a prisoner of war, home from his ordeal of near-starvation and mistreatment in a POW camp.

This shadow of a man—sunken eyes, sallow skin, and skeletal frame—was a far cry from my idea of a Prince Charming.

"Hazel," Lil said, "meet my brother, Robert."

My "Hi, Robert," was not acknowledged . . . he just kept shoveling scrambled eggs and toast in his mouth. "Oh, how rude. . . . " Slighted, I did an about face and left.

That introduction in the kitchen of the Respiratory Ward of 147th General Hospital was the first time I saw Robert—not a good first impression, and definitely not love at first sight.

Lil and I double-dated (with her arranging my dates)—none worth mentioning. Many times, I would stay over at Lil's, dress in her room, and leave for our dates. On my first sleepover, my "Hi, Robert," was acknowledged by brown eyes peering over newspaper and a nod.

Oh, well . . . so much for trying to be friendly.

Surprise. Surprise. Robert stopped by on his way to work at the Fort Shafter Motor Pool and asked me to a movie. "Sorry, I don't date servicemen." I did not share my reason—I was still trying to come to terms with my feelings. I knew of too many not-so-happy endings of wartime romances between local girls and servicemen.

~◊~

Three months later—another "just stopping by." Robert announced that he did not re-up so he was now a a civilian. He then asked whether I would like to go to the "Ice Follies" at the Honolulu International Center—our first date.

Many dates later—Chinese operas, Pirates of Penzance, movies, picnics, surfing, fishing, crabbing—and after many long hours of talking, I decided here was the man of my heart. Robert—a kind and honest man, a loving and caring man—was not a Prince Charming. He was my soul mate.

# SANDWICH, ANYONE?

He propped his fishing rod into the spike wedged between the planks on the boardwalk pier jutting out to sea at Sans Souci Beach. Splashes of salmon pink, fiery orange blending to mauve, and finally a blue-gray sky announced the coming of night.

He awoke to the terror of someone or something lying heavily on his chest and holding him down. Mr. Wong, a heavy-set man of 220 pounds, muscular, and in good physical condition from his younger years as an amateur boxer, could not get this "thing" off of him. The more he struggled, the heavier the "thing" became. A cold breath on his face froze him—now he could not move at all.

Feeling the weight suddenly lift off his prone body, all he could think of was, "Run, run. . . ." He tried to get on his feet to run, but all he could do was crawl along the boardwalk pier. Standing up on wobbly legs, he took a few steps, stumbled, and found himself on hands and knees again. This dance of the rag doll continued until hc finally got command of his legs—he staggered off the pier. Running across the sandy beach, the dry grass, and finally the hard cement sidewalk, he tore open the passenger door and took a flying dive into the front seat of his old Plymouth.

Next morning . . . everything was as he had abandoned the night before—rod and reel still propped in the spike, tackle box with cover open, and rain jacket wedged between the cracks in the boardwalk planks.

Except . . . flapping in the chilly morning breeze was a long piece of wax paper tied in the first eye of his fishing rod.   This piece of wax paper was wrapped around a sandwich that was supposed to be Mr. Wong's dinner the night before.

Roast pork sandwich . . . anyone?

~◊~

Mr. Wong told this spooky fishing story early one morning on our way to work at Tripler Army Medical Center.  We shared many fishing stories—this one was his spookiest.

# HONEYMOON COTTAGE

When Robert and I decided to get married, we received his mom's blessing and permission to build a small one-bedroom cottage in the area behind her house.

We toiled many months, cutting down haole koa bushes, digging out roots, and removing large rocks. One day, I saw a rounded rock that looked out of place—unnatural to the surrounding area. We dug up a huge blue rock with its center carved out—a water buffalo drinking trough. This rock was a keeper.

Our honeymoon cottage was completed one month before our June wedding date and was readied for us to move in.

~◊~

Our son, Bob, was born in July of the following year. When Bob was two years old we planned for another child. Bob asked for a baby sister.

When Rhonda was two years old, we decided to have our third child. Rhon wanted a baby sister. Anticipating our need for a larger place, we bought a 2-story house in Kalihi. We tried to have another baby for four long years . . . Aha, what we needed to do was to go back to our honeymoon cottage—the only place, it seemed, where I could get pregnant.

Mona was born two years later. Robert and I planned for a family of four—two boys and two girls—and we hoped Mona would ask for a baby brother. When asked, "Mona, would you like a brother or a sister . . .?"

"Oh . . . uh . . . I want a puppy. . . please."

# BEST PERFORMANCE OF THE YEAR

One dozen red roses! Never in my life had I received a dozen long-stemmed red roses.

Other flower arrangements came with congratulatory notes and best wishes. I was really taken with the one dozen long-stemmed red roses. "Hmmm . . . no card." I kept trying to guess who could afford such a beautiful, expensive arrangement. So extravagant—I love it.

The birth of our first-born, a son, was supposed to be on the 4$^{th}$ of July. My independence day came 12 days later. We named him Robert, after his father, of course. His middle name, Dale, (Dale Carnegie, *How to Make Friends and Influence People,*) we hoped would give him a name to live up to.

One dozen long-stemmed red roses . . . Who?

"Thanks, he's perfect." Ordinarily a man of few words, this time Robert was truly lost for words. "Here . . . I forgot. . . ."

The card, scrawled, "For the best performance of the year . . . Love, Robert."

# A GIRL ON GIRLS' DAY

Dr. William S. Ito, was our family doctor. He helped us give birth to our first son, and he was again here for us and our second child. He told me the estimated date of our baby's arrival would be March 3<sup>rd</sup>.

"Oh, great! I'm going to have a girl . . . a girl on Girls' Day."

Throughout my pregnancy I never doubted that I would have a daughter. From tiny booties to her patchwork quilt—everything was pink.

"A baby boy would really look silly in pink," Robert teased.

"Don't worry, she's going to look pretty in pink."

Although everything was "in the pink," I was not. I was green from nausea and vomiting, and I was not gaining weight as expected. Dr. Ito prescribed a protein granule supplement that I could not swallow, so he followed up with house calls every other day to give me B-12 injections. I was so depressed, I began having "the blues." Just about the time I began worrying about not being able to carry this pregnancy to term, I got up one morning . . . "I'm hungry."

~◊~

"For me?"

"Open it," Robert said.

"Thanks, Hon . . . a *Hina Matsuri* hime ningyo (Girls' Day princess doll). She's beautiful."

"She sure is . . . pretty in pink . . . like you said."

Our first daughter, Rhonda Lynn Ho, was born on Girls' Day, March 3, 1953.

# NEVER GO TO BED, ANGRY

"I'll never be poor again. . . . "

"You won't, I promise. . . ."

Robert and I were having our third round of whether or not I should go back to work. I was coming from growing up poor—going without the nicer things that my girlfriends had and I had not—sacrificing for my younger sisters and brothers because they needed something more. I took on the responsibility of housekeeping and childcare from an early age because my mom was sickly. I was overwhelmed by past feelings of resentment and fear of being trapped in poverty.

I knew Robert meant well. My dad, too, promised mom he would take care of her and the children, but it was impossible on only one paycheck. I was not going to let that happen to me, or my child.

For a month before I was scheduled to return to work, Robert and I talked in "Yes," "No," "Maybe," "Up to you," "If you like. . . ." It got so bad we reached a point where we were giving each other the silent treatment.

There were no more hugs and goodnight kisses—we slept with our backs to each other. I went to the bathroom to cry because I didn't want Robert to hear me.

The "Dear Abby" article was taped on my side of the bathroom mirror. It was about a couple that had had a terrible argument the night before and went to bed, angry. The following morning the wife discovered her dead husband and cried, "I'm sorry, I'm sorry. . . ."

I turned into Robert's arms. . . .

Robert choked, "I'm . . . sor . . . ry. . . ."
"I'm (sob) . . . sorry (sniff), too. . . ."

We promised each other we would never go to bed,
angry.

# SOUL MATES

The last of the lettuce seeds was put to bed. I stood up to straighten my back and felt the warmth of the morning sun on my face. Soybean, spinach, and squash seeds had already broken soil and were well on their way to our dinner table. "Let's take a break." As I handed him a glass of water, our hands touched, our eyes locked. . . .

"We've done this before. . . ."

"Yes, but this time we're doing it right."

~◊~

"Slowly, slowly, take your time," he coached. The bend in the rod told us that this was a big one. We had been salmon fishing for more than ten years and were still learning about the idiosyncrasies of salmon. With a sudden snap, the fish was gone—hook, lure, and dodger.

"Wow, second chance. Take your time, gently, slowly. . . ." When the salmon was finally netted and dropped into the fish box, our hands touched, our eyes locked. . . .

"We've done this before. . . ."

"Yes, but this time we're doing it right."

~◊~

How many times in this lifetime have our hands touched . . . our eyes locked. . . .

"We've done this before. . . ."

"Yes, but this time we're doing it right."

Soul mates.

Soul Mates
Hazel and Robert Ho
June 19, 1948, Church of the Crossroads

# THE EYES HAVE IT

Our eyes meet across a crowded room. My sideways glance catches Robert's eyes, and he knows it's time for us to leave the party.

When Bobby, Rhonda, and later, Mona were youngsters, they learned early that that certain look from Mom meant, "not another word." I never had to bribe or threaten them at the market or in stores to make them behave in an acceptable manner.

Bobby, our son, looked horrified when Uncle Sonny placed his beer can on the brand new koa coffee table—this, after Bobby had given him a beer glass and a coaster. Bobby's questioning look, "What do I do now?" All I needed to do was to give him "the eye," and he knew that he was not to say or do anything. Later, when he asked why I had done nothing, I told him that Uncle Sonny was a guest in our home, and we would treat him like one.

"Mom, everybody's going, even Linda's mom said, 'okay'," Rhonda, argued. Linda stood behind Rhonda, nodding.
"Rhonda, you are not everybody, and I am not Linda's mom. . . ."
"Oh, mom, please, please. . . ."

I gave Rhonda "the eye." She got the message. She stopped begging.

Eye signals—the "only joking" wink, the "oh, no, not again" upward eyeball roll, the "time to leave this party" sideways glance, the "I said, no" glare—among family members who learned, understood, and shared them were very effective nonverbal communication.

# CHRISTMAS, EVERY DAY

Life with Robert is Christmas, every day.

The first year we were married, Robert bought me a two-piece bathing suit—no, not a bikini—I loved it.

When our son Bob was born, Robert and I agreed that we would stop giving each other store bought gifts and give to our child instead. We continued this agreement with gifts for our daughters, Rhonda and Ramona. We taught our children the difference between a need and a want. Their needs were met, but when there was something special they wanted, they would have to work and save their own money to pay for half the cost. For Christmas, however, we would give each child one gift that they wanted.

For myself, all I need to do is open my heart to receive Robert's gifts—not only at Christmas—all year round. His gifts were always a labor of love. Simple, everyday gifts—relocating a spigot in the yard so I wouldn't fall over it, marketing for fresh ingredients to cook a special dinner for me, helping with care of the children, sacrificing six oranges when he cut a branch of orange blossoms and placed it in an old soy bottle on the breakfast table. His most recent gift—he planted an avocado tree. This, he did to give me "hope" of seeing and tasting the fruit. "Just stick with me, kiddo, the best is yet to come."

Each year, when the family gets together for Christmas dinner, Robert and I catch each other's eyes and smile. We are enjoying the best Christmas gifts we have given each other—three of them—Bob, Rhon and Mona.

Christmas, every day!

Rhonda Lynn, Robert Dale, Ramona Anne
Our Forever Christmas Gifts

"She Chinee . . . not Japanee."
"She not Buddha . . . she Cat . . .lic . . . what that?"
"No, no, no can marry," Grandpa Arii objected.
Grandma shook her head, "Ikenai, ikenai (unacceptable).
Uncle Takeo married her anyway.

Aunty "Momoyo" received her Japanese name from Grandpa, who reluctantly accepted his Chinese, Catholic daughter-in-law into the household, but not in his heart.

Aunty Momoyo soon learned not only the household routine, but learned to speak Japanese so she could understand what was being said to her, and about her. She learned Grandpa's likes and dislikes, catered to his every whim, and endeared herself to Grandpa and to the rest of the family.

Grandpa would ask Aunty Momoyo to cook special Japanese dishes for him—nishime (cooked vegetables), kimpira (burdock roots), and shrimp and vegetable tempura (deep fried). He stopped going to the barbershop—only Aunty Momoyo cut his hair just the way he liked it. Every now and then Grandpa would sneak spending money to Aunty Momoyo.

It was Aunty Momoyo who took care of Grandpa while he recuperated at home between gallbladder surgeries. His surgical site would not heal. I believe Grandpa's non-healing surgical site was because of undiagnosed diabetes—a little known condition during his time. Aunty Momoyo was his 24-hour nurse.

One night when Aunty Momoyo was spoon feeding miso soup to Grandpa, I heard him say, "Momoyo, you my best Japanese daughter-in-law. . . ." Blinded by tears, she missed Grandpa's open mouth and spilled miso soup all over his pajamas. "Aiyaahh, Momoyo," Grandpa yelped, then both burst out laughing, as Aunty Momoyo clumsily wiped the wetness off Grandpa's clothes with a dish towel. Hiding behind the half open bedroom door, I cried and laughed with them.

~◊~

Years later, this Japanese girl married into a Chinese family. At my wedding reception, Uncle Takeo said, "It'll be easier for you and Robert, than it was for me and Aunty Momoyo."

Many more years later, I overheard Popo tell our next door neighbor, Mrs. Ching, "Hazel . . . my best Chinese daughter-in-law. . . ."

Uncle Takeo, son Gilbert, and Aunty Momoyo

# CALL ME, "POPO"

"Call me, 'Popo'," she said, so, Popo she was from the first time I met her when my friend Lillian introduced me to her mom. Little did I know at the time that this mild-mannered Chinese woman was soon to be my mother-in-law.

~◊~

Go Moi Lee was born in Hawaii, the second of seven children of Gee Lee and Yuen Moi Chew. At about age two, she left for China with her mother and grandparents and lived in the Yu Hung Lai Village near Macau. She returned to Honolulu at age twelve.

At age 18, Go Moi married Lim Ho. My husband, Robert was one of her eight children, the youngest of her three sons. A young widow, she raised her children by selling seed craft to tourists in Waikiki. She spent hours gathering seeds, drilling holes in the seeds, and creating beautiful earrings, necklaces, bracelets and handbags. A most remarkable thing about Popo was the fact that she did all this with vision in only one eye. She had lost her right eye to a soda bottle cap.

~◊~

Popo made life easy for her Japanese daughter-in-law. From the very beginning she cooked dinners for us on Monday nights when she found out we went for a swim after work. She always seemed to cook too much and would bring us "left-over" food. She shared Chinese "goodies" whenever she returned from marketing and would not accept our offers to pay. Popo was always kind to me and for that I am forever grateful. But more than that, "Popo, 'thank you' for raising my wonderful husband."

# SEVEN-ELEVENS

"Wow, seven-elevens!"

No, we're not at the craps tables in Las Vegas.

Dad was at my front door delivering his fresh catch of the day—seven-eleven crabs. His love for fishing was so great, he continued even after he underwent a tracheostomy for cancer of the esophagus.

As a teenager, I thought nothing I did pleased him. I tried so hard because he was the only one of his brothers who had a girl for his firstborn. I competed with my boy cousins—outrun, out-swim, out-fish—always trying to outdo them Once I was grounded for one week for beating my cousin Henry with a bamboo sword while practicing kendo.

The proudest day spent with dad was the rainy day when I beat him to the reef at Ala Moana Beach. He swam, always two strokes behind me, never letting up. "You were just lucky," he said. Hmmm . . . did he let me win? I don't think so. . . .

Everyone had already gone into the tents. Dad and I took the first watch. We talked fishing—his favorite talk. A sudden pained look on his face told me he was hurting from an old back injury he had suffered when his overloaded truck flipped into a ditch on Kunia Road. I began massaging his back—Hawaiian lomi-lomi style. He said in Japanese, "Kay, you've grown up to be a pretty good human being."

Was I a rotten kid? Not. . . .

All throughout my growing up years, Dad minimized his compliments. "Not bad . . . could be better . . . try again. . . ." Never, "Great job, the best. . . ." I had to try harder, always try harder.

Today, as dad handed me the crabs, "Kay, my best seven-elevens . . . for you . . . the best."

"Wow, Dad . . . Thanks."

# BIG BROTHER

Bob needed an Aloha shirt and Rhon needed a muu muu for their May Day Program at Liholiho Elementary School.

"I can only afford one . . . Aloha shirt or muumuu?"

"Let Rhon have her muumuu. It's her first May Day Program. Besides, girls need a new dress more than boys need a shirt. I can wear one of my old Aloha shirts . . . no big thing." This was the loving and giving decision that Bob made at age nine.

Bob is a caring and giving person. Throughout the years—upgrading cars so his sisters will be driving newer and safer cars, paying private school tuition and fees for his niece (Rhon's daughter Jessica), salmon fishing trips for his sister Mona—his generosity has been overwhelming.

Bob does not give only on the material level. He is patient and kind, and gives of his time and energy. When they have questions, ask his opinion, or seek his advice, he makes time for his sisters.

Robert and I feel blessed and comforted knowing that Bob will always be there for his sisters. Our daughters are so fortunate . . . they have a big brother.

# AQUARIUM

"Today, we're going to the aquarium. . . ."
"Oh, good, Daddy, I love fish."

Soon, Rhonda found herself surrounded by the stink of fish, shrimp, Kona crabs, and spiny lobster.

"But Daddy, I thought you said we were going to the aquarium."
"That's right, Rhon, this is an aquarium . . . the dead aquarium."
"Oh, Daddy, you so funny."

Marketing in Chinatown was a new experience for five-year-old Rhon. Pinching her nose with her left thumb and forefinger, her right hand lifting and turning the fish, she checked the eyes of kumu, weke, aweoweo and menpachi— clear eyes, buy; cloudy eyes, no buy. Her favorite was Kona crabs that she bought only if they were frothing at the mouth and moving.

~◊~

Today, when marketing for fresh seafood, Rhon always goes to Chinatown.
"Dad, you want to go to the dead aquarium?"

# A DOG'S BEST FRIEND

Mona sat on the floor of the pet store, hugging the small, brown puppy, refusing to let go. She insisted, "I don't want a baby brother or a baby sister, I want a baby puppy, please?" Twenty-five dollars for a puppy was too much for our budget. Mona begged to do extra chores to pay for her half of Rusty's cost.

Rusty, our new "baby," came home on Mona's 7th birthday.

~◊~

Just short of sleeping in the doghouse with him, Mona and Rusty were inseparable. When it was time to go to school in the morning, it was tough on both of them. At the sound of the last bell, Mona would run the two blocks from school to home to her anxiously waiting puppy. Rusty would tip his head slightly to the left, cock his right ear and look attentively at Mona. He was always rewarded for his good behavior with "good boy," a scratch behind his ears or a tiny snack. There were times when I wondered who was training whom.

~◊~

Brothers would sometimes find a new home with our family when we didn't have the heart to leave just one behind. There were always at least two, sometimes three, happy poi dog faces with tongues and tails wagging to greet us when we returned home at the end of each day. Through the years, Rusty and his pals, Sandy, Toby, Coco, Blackie, Zeus, Apollo, Spot, Jet, Lucky, Sam and Oscar took very good care of our children.

~◊~

A loyal child . . . a dog's best friend.

# THE BEST CHRISTMAS TREE IN THE WORLD

"Look, Mom, look at our tree.  It's going to be the best Christmas tree in the world," Mona beamed, as she held the very top of the tree she thought she was helping to carry. Her sister, Rhon, carried the load in the center and big brother, Bob, carried the brunt of the six-foot Douglas fir.

Well, I did say that they could have a Christmas tree only as big as the three of them could carry off the lot.  It was a good-looking tree—fresh green needles, thick, bushy branches evenly spread out. . . .  "Oh, no, look at the top . . . it's crooked.  Why didn't you check the top?"

Bob looked at Rhon and shrugged. Rhon tilted her head towards Mona. "Mom, I saw the top," Mona said.  "I knew it was crooked. But Mom, if we didn't buy this tree, nobody else would, and it would never be a Christmas tree."

Christmas music in the background, we began decorating our tree—origami birds, egg carton ornaments, seven special Hallmark ornaments for Mona, thirteen for Rhon, and seventeen for Bob —all precious mementos of Christmas.

Robert lifted Mona as she reached up, slightly to the right.  I couldn't tell which shone brighter . . . my little angel, or the one she placed on the crooked treetop.

"Behold, 'The Best Christmas Tree in the World'."

# NEW YEAR'S EVE AT POPO'S

Delicious juk was the highlight of New Year's Eve at Popo's. Popo would begin by boiling a whole chicken in the largest pot in her kitchen. Later, she added rice, ground pork, and the so-called "good stuff." The "good stuff" consisted of pig guts, chicken livers, gizzards, and hearts. Marble-sized fish cake balls were dropped into the hot soup just before serving, so they would be cooked perfectly tender.

Popo insisted everyone eat juk as the first meal of the New Year for "good luck." "This small pot juk special for Hazel," she announced, when she found out I would not eat her juk with all the "good stuff." "Nobody eat this one . . . only for Hazel, no mo' pig gut. . . ."

It was also "tradition" for the family to get together for firecracker tying. Spreading newspapers on Popo's living room floor, family members would bring out many boxes of thousands of firecrackers. Layers upon layers of firecrackers were tied together with cotton strings into long, 20-foot lengths. When the aunties with cigarettes hanging from their lips came out of the kitchen to the living room, everyone would yell, "Aunty, go outside!"

By the time her living room was cleaned up and the last firecracker was popped, Popo had already ladled the first meal of the New Year into small bowls for her many grandchildren. She let the juk cool off a bit, "so no burn mouth," she cautioned.

~◊~

Before the sun rises on the morning of New Year's Eve, Robert already has a whole chicken boiling in the pot.

# DON'T BRING ME FLOWERS WHEN I'M DEAD

People visit the resting places of their departed loved ones—placing flowers on the graves, tossing leis in the ocean. Some even have family picnics at the cemeteries. I don't. It's not that I don't remember . . . I do—my way.

I remember Dad—I always bought him poke (seasoned raw fish) and beer when he was alive. Dad brought me flowers—a red hibiscus, a double pikake (jasmine), lilikoi (passion fruit) flowers, and mountain apple blossoms.

Memories of Mom and my sister Sets—I bought them clay pots, cinder, and fertilizer. When I saw a beautiful orchid plant, I bought three—one for Mom, one for Sets, and one for me. Sets did the same. On Sunday afternoons we sat on the grass in the shade of Sets' garage and potted orchids. We talked about our families, our jobs, and our futures. The three of us promised we would remember these "potting times" when it came to "parting time" and agreed: "Don't bring me flowers when I'm dead."

With each piece of sphagnum moss I pressed down around the roots of my Minho Princess . . . I remember Sets. Fragrance of honohono blossoms . . . I remember Mom. Harvesting lilikoi from my backyard . . . I remember Dad.

~◊~

| | |
|---|---|
| Flower Shop Lady: | Who you buying these flowers for?" |
| Mona: | "They're for my mom." |
| Flower Shop Lady: | "Oh, these flowers too delicate for graveyard . . . you take red gingers instead . . . last mo' longer." |
| Mona: | "My mom is not dead, she's alive." |
| Flower Shop Lady: | "Oh, you good girl . . . I wish my children bring me flowers. . . ." |

~◊~

The best part about "giving" flowers to loved ones while they're still alive—their happy smiles—is the instant "receiving" of joy and happiness for yourself.

Today is Memorial Day, 1998. I received beautiful blue irises from my daughter Mona.

# GOODBYE, "PATCHES"

A 7 feet x 7 feet patchwork quilt, made of 3 inch x 3 inch squares of scrap materials left over from Aloha shirts, was named "Patches" by our son, Bob. Grandma, who did piece work—sewing parts of Aloha shirts—gave Patches to Bob when he was five years old, to take to school on his first day of kindergarten. "This 'blankie' too big," the teacher said, so it was sent home. This was okay with Bob, because he didn't want to put Patches on the dirty classroom floor.

Laundry day was always stressful. Patches was the first load on the clothesline. Bob would spend time sitting on the laundry basket and waiting, hoping Patches would dry before day's end. On stormy nights when the wind howled, thunder shook his bed, and lightning cast scary shadows on his bedroom walls, Patches covered Bob's head. When Bob came home from the hospital, after having his appendix removed, Patches hugged him.

Patches got smaller as Bob grew bigger—from a 7 feet x 7 feet quilt to a 5 feet x 5 feet quilt with many repairs and replacement of the edges. Soon, Patches was cut down to a 3 feet x 3 feet quilt with patches on the patchwork pieces. Finally, too small for the bed, and looking more like a rug than a quilt, Patches ended on the bedroom floor as cushion for Bob's barbells and weights.

The "click-clicks" of snipping scissors were the only sounds late that night. A short haircut was the last of Bob's "to do" things before leaving for Schofield Barracks in the morning.  His unit had been activated and he was ordered to report for training on the mainland and, later, for duty in Viet Nam.  Remembering Bob's first haircut—sitting on his dad's lap and crying in protest—streams of tears flowed with each lock of long, black hair I dropped to the bathroom floor.

I tried to make light of the situation by teasing, "Bob, are you going to take Patches with you . . .?"  Silence.

Later, I heard Bob, "Goodbye, Patches.  Thanks for being there for me. . . .  Sorry, I can't take you with me . . . I'm not going camping. . . . This time it's for real."

"Goodbye . . . Patches. . . ."

PFC Robert Dale Ho

Robert, Bob, Hazel

# RETURN ON INVESTMENTS

"Dad, I need your help."

This would not be the first time one of our children would ask for help. Our philosophy has always been: We wanted them, we are responsible for them and to them, and they are the best investments of our time and money. So, it was no surprise to hear our son ask his dad for help, again. Bob needed his dad to help him drive a car home. This one was easy.

A white Mercury Sable station wagon driven by Robert, came to a stop in front of our garage. Bob beamed, "It's yours, Dad."

We had been talking about needing a replacement car but had been stalling the inevitable. We were overwhelmed. Never have we ever had such a luxurious car. We always had to settle for used, compact cars—affordable ones.

Tears welled. Robert seemed frozen at the steering. I lowered myself into a lawn chair.

"Thanks, Dad, Mom, for 90 years of encouragement and support. "

"90 years?"

"Yes, I'm 45 years old. Multiply that by two great parents. . . ."

I always knew our children were the best investments we ever made.

# SMOKE-FREE FACILITY

A long drag from my Virginia Slims cigarettes instantly launched me into a coughing spell that just wouldn't quit. I choked on the water I thought would clear my throat and started another round of coughing, wheezing and retching. Runners-by just ran by—some without a second look, while others just stared and kept on running. Embarrassed, I put out the cigarette on the grass. I turned my back to the running path and continued to cough.

"Girlie, you okay? You want water?" asked an elderly Hawaiian tutu (grandmother) who stopped to check on me.

"Thank you, Aunty. I'll be okay . . . it's just my cigarette cough. . . ."

This coughing spell was the hardest and longest of my cigarette coughs. I thought, how stupid . . . you're out of breath from running, and you smoked a cigarette. . . . Do you want to run, or do you want to smoke? You can't do both. Make up your mind.

I made up my mind. I remember that day—January 25, 1983. I've made New Year's resolutions to quit smoking too many times. I could never do it. It was too late for a New Year's resolution, anyway. This time, I decided I would give myself a birthday present . . . "Happy Birthday to me."

Lil introduced me to the "guys and gals" soon after I began working with her at the 147th General Hospital across from Fort Shafter. She became my big sister and I was grateful to her for being my best friend and mentor. She introduced me to "Lucky" in the bathroom of the Blue Moon nightclub. Lil said that I looked too young and innocent and that I should at least hold a cigarette and puff on it. My first puff of Lucky Strike cigarettes was a disaster. I thought I was going to die . . . Lil thought I was going to die. Lil took me home.

My nicotine experiment began with occasional trials of 1-2 cigarettes a day that I had bummed off of Lil. Lil finally said, "buy your own. . . ." The 1-2 packs a day habit escalated to a 2-3 packs a day addiction.

To my credit—if I can call it that—I did quit smoking for long periods. Each time I became pregnant, I quit smoking during the nine months of pregnancy and during the three months of nursing my babies. So, I could have stopped smoking those three times.

My excuse? Smoking relieved the stresses of work. With mounting work stresses—personnel changes, budget cuts, promotions, and added responsibilities—I found myself lighting up more and more. I joked about my ashtray smoking more than I did.

I retired.

~◊~

The Honolulu Marathon as my goal, I began my healthy lifestyle with changes in diet, an exercise program, and meditation.

After three months, beginning with short, slow walks, followed by speed walking, I was ready for jogging. It was on my first attempt at jogging that I suffered my scary coughing episode described at the beginning of this story.

A just-opened pack of Virginia Slims was crushed and tossed into a trash bin on my way back to the car. I announced my decision to Robert . . . "Okay," he said, "we'll give it a try. . . ."

~◊~

I sat in my favorite chair with a pitcher of ice water. Watching TV, I found myself reaching for my cigarettes. Oh, I forgot, no more cigarettes. Okay, take another sip of ice water. . . .

The first three days of my stop smoking campaign were painful. I had the shakes—my fingers trembled, my hands jerked—and my head ached.

To satisfy my urge to put something in my mouth, I ate potato chips with chopsticks—the chopsticks being kept between my lips longer than necessary. Knitting and crocheting kept my hands busy—Afghans, scarves, beanies, pullovers, cardigans, blouses, skirts, hot pants, Argyles.

Withdrawal symptoms became less during the following three weeks. I kept drinking ice water. . . . No coffee—coffee and cigarettes go together.

~◊~

Oh, no, I lit a cigarette . . . quick, put it out . . . aww shucks, there goes my quit smoking . . . guess, I better just forget about it. I sat up in bed and was happy this scenario was just a dream. I had many such recurrent dreams—a cigarette in one hand and a cup of coffee in the other; talking on the phone between long nicotine drags; lighting up after a meal—each time awakening with relief that I was only dreaming.  The dreams, too, became less as the months and years passed.

~◊~

I ran the Honolulu Symphony Run three consecutive years, and the Pepsi 10K, twice.  The Honolulu Marathon? Not yet. . . .

Today, I am a smoke-free facility . . . 24 years and counting. . . .

# YOUNG DOCTOR BRIGID

Brigid Maile Ho, born June 3, 1980, our first granddaughter, is a caring and loving child. As a youngster, she worried about grandma's feelings and well-being. Brigid liked to play "doctor" whenever grandma was not feeling well.

Brigid found me in bed one day with a migraine. Following a cursory physical examination—"open your mouth," "stick out your tongue," and feeling my forehead— she asked, "How are you feeling now?"

"Mrs. Ho," Brigid said, "you'll be feeling well in no time. . . ." The following "doctors orders," scrawled on a piece of lined folder paper, was handed to me.

Patient:  Hazel K. Ho
Complaint:  Head ake . . . very bad.
               Complanes it is to hot for her.
Treatment:  2:00 PM  Need ice pack on head.
               2:35 PM  Should bc feeling a little better.
               Keep ice pack on and off about each 5 minutes.
               Open windows . . . rest . . . lay down.
               Need peice and quite.
Dr. Brigid Ho      Date:  8/3/88
Fee:  $5.00 Cash Only

Brigid Maile,  Age 8

*GRANDPA'S GARDEN*

*Shy turtles hide among the ancient papyrus*
*Peeking out to greet an old friend,*
*Blessings from heaven reflect a prism of colors,*
*The old man smiles.*

*Golden lilies kiss a flawless surface*
*Fairies, in a surreal dream,*
*Dragonflies dart across the pond*
*As quick as skipping stones*
*Fleeting like a heart reborn,*
*The old man smiles.*

*Fragrant orange blossoms hang heavy*
*In the pristine spring breeze,*
*My Grandpa smiles.*

*Happy Birthday, Grandpa*
*11/12/03*
*Love, Jessica Jo*

# ONE MAN, TWO HANDS, MILLIONS OF SEEDS

As a young boy, his father taught him about the seasons, the soil, and the seeds. He cleared plot after plot of bushes and large boulders from his parents' land. The physical labor strengthened his body, but his commitment to the land is what transformed this boy into a man. He learned to produce food from the earth.

His strong, callused, yet gentle hands have pressed millions of seeds into the earth. His trees produce sweet oranges, papayas, mangoes, figs, bananas, and buttery avocados. From his vines, hang juicy red flame grapes, beans, tomatoes, and squashes of every shape, size, and color. Fresh root ginger, chives, and green onions spice our family recipes, year-round. Marigolds plant themselves throughout the garden.

When garden pests helped themselves to some of his crop, he doesn't try to kill them. "They have to eat, too." he says, "I just have to plant a little bit more."

He generously shares his abundance with family, friends, and all of his neighbors.

Sixty year ago, Robert planted a seed of love in my heart.

# LADY OF THE LAKE

I stopped only briefly to take a closer look at a tiny, white flower on the side of the path. When I looked up, I realized I had been left behind. There were no voices or sounds of footsteps ahead or behind me on the trail. I was alone.

A heavy mist advanced toward me. Pulling my hood over my head, I hurried to join the group ahead.

A sudden chill and an eerie feeling came over me. I looked up from under my hood and saw a tall, dark shadow standing on the boardwalk that went almost to the center of the lake. Straining to get a better look, I could make out a hooded, black-caped figure. I thought about joining that person to see what was so interesting in the lake. . . . She turned around and smiled. The smile was frozen on her face, and I froze on the spot.

It seemed every time I looked back, she was getting closer—behind a tree, behind a bush, behind me—always behind me. I could hardly breathe, and I feared my wobbly legs would give out from under me. I kept running . . . straight into big, strong arms holding me tightly around my waist.

Screaming, "Help, somebody, help me . . ," and kicking, I kept beating the hands that caught me . . . "Let me go . . . let go. . . ."

"Hey, it's me . . . what's wrong? You're shaking. No wonder, you're wet . . . must be cold." Robert, who came looking for me, wrapped his raincoat around me.

I looked back to see if the lady was still behind me. Where did she go?

Later, as the group gathered to get back on board, I looked for a lady in a long, hooded cape. No, no lady in black.

I will never forget the lady of the lake—her smile—she haunts me till this day.

# SNAGGED IN THE EYE

My fishing buddy, Robert, and I were trolling in a zig-zag pattern heading to "The Point." The loud screaming of my reel and line being stripped from the spool signaled a Silver salmon had taken my lure and started its high speed run. Of the five Pacific salmon, Silvers are the feistiest. They will jump, twist, turn and run, slack, and tangle your dodger or sinker in a last ditch attempt to throw the hook.

After approximately twenty minutes of acrobatics on the part of both salmon and angler, a sudden slack in my line caused brief anxiety. "Did I lose him?" I frantically reeled in my line. Suddenly, my line became taut. The Silver ran under the skiff in its last attempt for freedom. Guiding my rod to the opposite side of the skiff, I continued to retrieve line. Soon, the white underside of the Silver told me it had bellied up and was ready to be netted.

"I can't believe this . . . Hon, you've got to see this one." Robert leaned over the fish box and shook his head in disbelief. The first of my tandem hooks was dangling outside of the Silver's lower jaw. However, my second trailing hook had snagged the eye—no, not the eye of the salmon—the eye of a treble hook embedded on the opposite side of the lower jaw. This Silver had apparently gotten away from a previous angler and was unlucky enough to be caught by me in this most amazing manner.

"Hello, Silver, welcome aboard."

Fishing Buddies

This story previously appeared in the book:
*The Salmon Fishing Adventure:*
*How to Locate, Lure and Land the Big Salmon and More...*
www.salmonfishingadventure.com

# CRY TOMORROW

"Cry tomorrow," Mom said, "tomorrow, it won't be so bad . . . you'll see, it's not the end of the world. And, maybe, tomorrow there'll be nothing to cry about."

I stopped crying. . . . I started thinking about how I would face and answer my accuser, her mom, my teacher, and the principal. I was being accused of stealing lunch money from Sally, my best friend.

Tomorrow came. During the meeting, it turned out that Sally had misplaced her lunch money in one of the many pockets in her school bag. Apologies accepted. Mom was right. Lesson learned: Cry tomorrow . . . tomorrow you may have nothing to cry about.

When life threw me a curve, I remembered mom's wisdom, "Cry tomorrow."

There was one time, however, "Cry tomorrow" did not work. The anxiety of waiting for a pathology report of a biopsy—malignant or non-malignant—of a "suspicious" mass on my left breast discovered on a mammogram was too much . . . I cried.

The anger of "why me?" when told I may need a mastectomy was too much . . . I cried.

Horror stories of adverse effects of chemotherapy and radiation therapy left me in despair . . . I cried.

I feared that tomorrow may never come . . . I cried.

As time passed, I realized there would be many more tomorrows. I was blessed with a supportive family—a husband who loved me even when I was bald. He made me laugh. "Now we can save money," he said, "No need go beauty shop." Bob, Rhon, and Mona took turns bringing potluck meals, doing laundry, and helping with housework.

"Cry tomorrow...." Works for me.

# *YUREI:* GHOST

The *Yurei* of Japanese movies almost always waded out of the river from under a willow tree. The specter— white ashen face, long straggly hair, and red, sunken eyes— would glare threateningly and wail words of vengeance upon those who had poisoned her.

The *Yurei* in the mirror was me. I was pale as a ghost, with straggly hair, and eyes red from crying. Clumps of wet hair stuck on my comb, more in my hands, and still more lay on the bathroom floor. Yes, I too, had been poisoned—chemotherapy.

Diagnosed early, Stage 1 breast cancer, the treatment of choice was a lumpectomy, to be followed by chemotherapy and radiation therapy. Nausea and vomiting kept me off my feet for days following each chemotherapy treatment. Loss of appetite did not help. I kept losing weight till I looked like a scarecrow.

Enough!

I decided I didn't have to look like a *yurei.* I bought two wigs no more cover-up scarves or hats for me. Makeup was another story—seemed to take longer to put on my makeup. Okay, now the lipstick . . . Oh, oh, time out. Back from the bathroom, I continued painting a presentable face. Oops, missed my upper lip . . . wipe off the lipstick from my nose . . . try again.

Look better . . . feel better . . . way to go.

The skin on my left breast looked like I had left my top off, fell asleep, and had gotten badly sunburned. Luckily, a prescription ointment precluded any infection. Considering my immune system had been highly compromised when twenty-two lymph nodes were removed at the time of my lumpectomy, radiation therapy was not so bad.

At first, small areas of "fuzz" began to peek from the top of my head, the back, and the sides. Soon I could grab thick clumps of hair with each shampoo. My hair was growing, no longer falling out. Wigs came off after my first visit to Susan. She gave me a stylish pixie haircut. "You look younger," Robert said.

Throughout this ordeal, I was blessed with a family who made me feel needed—a husband who catered to my every need; yet, allowed me to cook meals on my "good days." Robert made me see the funny side of life, and we shared something to laugh about every day. I am so lucky to have him.

"Mom, look what I did. . . . Mom, what do you think? Mom, should I . . .?" My three grown children—who shared their everyday triumphs and tribulations—made me feel needed and lucky to be alive.

Did I say I am lucky? Yes . . . I am lucky.

I am not a *Yurei*. . . .

I am a Survivor!

# AUTUMN OF MY BALD EAGLE

"Screee, screee." Baldy had seen my white baseball cap waving above my head. He flew off his perch—the top of the highest evergreen on his island— and began gliding down toward my skiff. With wings widely spread and his sharp talons open, he floated slowly down. Silently flying low over the water, he suddenly snatched a small pink salmon swimming close to the surface. Circling my skiff with an earsplitting "scree, scree," he skimmed the water and headed back to his island. Gracefully touching down on a dry branch of a beached log, he released his catch and began enjoying his breakfast. My time with Baldy, seven days in autumn, was the highlight of my annual salmon fishing adventure.

"This may be the last time I'll be seeing you, Baldy." Hot tears streaked down my cold cheeks, joining rivulets from my nose, and dripping off my chin. Wiping my chin with the back of a gloved hand, I took off my wig to show Baldy that I was the bald one. "Look, look at me, look who's calling who, baldy?" Hair loss was one of the side effects of chemotherapy.

Nausea, loss of appetite, and lack of energy were also adverse effects of treatment. I was not one to allow these minor setbacks to prevent me from living my life on my own terms. Negotiating an acceptable chemotherapy schedule with my oncologist, armed with painkillers and over-the-counter drugs, I was able to keep my date with Baldy.

This year I was happy just to be here, sitting in my skiff enjoying the tangerine-fuchsia Ketchikan sunrise with Baldy. Later, I will go looking for Ping and Pong, the otters who play hide and seek among the kelp just before the cliffs of Betton Island. I may be lucky to see the resident orcas—mom and her sons— of Clover Passage, who frequent the waters between Revillagigedo and Gravina Islands. I'll look for auklets and gulls—they tell me where the Silver salmon are feeding. The water ballet of harbor porpoises entertains me until I hear the screaming of line letting out from my reel, reminding me that I'm supposed to be fishing. I look forward to a wine-mauve Ketchikan sunset—all the while being thankful for one more autumn with my Baldy.

My fishing adventures were never just for the sport or the fish. My curious nature has always led me to inquire, explore, or investigate all that this land has to offer. I have had the good fortune to know and appreciate: The friendly people—each with their unique heritage and culture; Denali's majestic beauty mirrored in a lake created by a dam that took generations of beaver families to build—one aspen branch at a time; the many misty fjords; calving glaciers; the lure of gold, panning the river beds of the Eldorado Canyon in Kantishna; treks through the back country, while cautiously looking for signs of wolf tracks in the freshly fallen snow; moose munching on tender willow shoots, a grizzly napping in the shade of a vein of twisted alder and more. . . .

Of all the majesty and beauty of Alaska, I am most humbled by the myriad creatures that share His creation with us. Of His creatures, I am most inspired by the bald eagle that is, to me, the epitome of strength, power, and gracefulness.

The hope of maybe, just maybe, seeing Baldy—same time, same place—next autumn has given me the strength to complete the remainder of my chemotherapy treatment.

I have the power to choose—radiation therapy for six weeks? Whatever happens, I can accept what is to be.

One day in autumn, I will soar home to Him on the wings of Baldy, my graceful bald eagle. . . .

But not today. …

This story previously appeared in the book:
*The Salmon Fishing Adventure:*
*How to Locate, Lure, and Land The Big Salmon and More.* .
.
www.salmonfishingadventure.com

"Baldy," my Bald Eagle

Bald Eagle (Haliaeetus leucocephalus)

Adult Weight: Up to 14 pounds (average 9 pounds)
Females larger than males

Wing Span: 6-8 feet across
Swoops and dives as fast as 200 miles per hour

Life Span: About 20 years in the wild
Diurnal: Hunts during day; sleeps at night

Nests on tall trees near bodies of water
Monogamous for life; share raising their young
until eaglets leave nest (about 12 weeks)

# A TALE OF TWO WHALES
## A Close Encounter of the Awesome Kind


A dark shadow beneath my skiff struck fear in my heart. There was an eerie silence.

My heart began pounding out $32^{nd}$ notes. In one synchronized movement—to port, a black dorsal fin rose straight up from the water to a height that seemed the width of my skiff, and starboard, another fin twice as large shaded the sun—two monsters of the sea sandwiched my small skiff. A tidal wave of primal fear engulfed my whole being.

Trapped between a mother orca and her adult son, I lost myself in self-centered thoughts of my own mortality. "Oh, God, is today the day? Well, I . . . ah, okay. . . ." The moment I accepted His will, I felt a calming peace wash over me.

Mother Orca and son slowly raised their heads and flippers above the water to spy on us . . . then on with the show. Leaping high out of the water, they splashed noisily down into the water on their stomachs, sides, and backs. Their flipper slapping—as if to applaud their own performance—was accompanied by my clapping. After many encores, Mother Orca rolled slowly on her side and slapped her dorsal fin on the surface of the water—a loud boom and "Old Faithful"—a grand finale.

Two waving flippers melted into concentric rings created by raindrops on the surface of the dark waters. I closed my eyes and a balm of tears and raindrops moisturized my face.

"It's not your time. . . ," Ojiisan whispered. . . .

~157~

This close encounter of the awesome kind comforts and sustains me.

Mother Orca and son

This story previously appeared in the book:
*The Salmon Fishing Adventure:*
*How to Locate, Lure, and Land the Big Salmon and More. . .*
www.salmonfishingadventure.com

# LESSONS FROM MY ARBOR

I always wanted a grape vine.

My earliest memory of a grapevine is "borrowing" blue grapes from Aunty Konno's neighbor's yard. My sister Sets, cousin Dora, and I would reach over the fence and grab as many grapes as we could pull off from the clusters. I can still taste the tartness as I peeled the skin between my teeth, and the gush of sweet grape juice as I bit into the flesh. I didn't know much about grapes then, but I believe they were Concords. The neighbor knew exactly what was happening to his grapes—clusters along that part of the fence were left on the vine.

The ad in the newspaper read, "Seedless Red Flame Grapes." I called to find out whether these were table grapes or wine grapes—goes to show how little I knew about grapes. I was not interested in wine grapes. Being told the plants were table grapes, my yearning for a grape vine was intensified. I asked the garden shop clerk to hold three plants for me.

Robert and I took a ride to the windward side of the island. There were three healthy plants in 6-inch pots, with tendrils clinging on to each other. It was meant for me to take these three, as they were not about to let go of each other.

"Oh, no! What happened?" Oh, my poor grape plants—leaves that were so green and healthy just last evening were now lacy and turning brown. Something ate my grape plants last night. I called the University of Hawaii

Department of Agriculture Diagnostic Services, and was told that my problem was "rose beetles." You have to catch them beetles for about three nights or so until you catch the local population. Hmm, I remember those guys, they were the ones who, several years ago, tatted the leaves on my rose plants into intricate lacework. I lost that battle of the roses to those nasty beetles.

Robert was the designer. Bob and Mona were the builders. They are only carpenters in their hearts and not by trade, so their labor of love took seven days. Rhonda, Brigid, and Jessica took on beetle patrol. The grape arbor became a family affair.

"Grandma, I got another one. Oh, oh, they're on me. Eeeeyah. . . ." Jess was jumping up and down and spinning round and round, brushing off beetles that were attracted to the flashlight in her hand.

"Jess, stop screaming or the beetles are going to fly in your mouth."

"Okay, grandma."

On the first night, the beetle patrol captured fifty-seven rose beetles that we put into the peanut butter jar of soap water. So, we had two more nights of the battle of the beetles? I am not about to give up on my grape vines. I'm up for the challenge and I intend to win this war. I will taste the sweet flesh of my red flame grapes. . . .

It didn't take long for the three replacement grape vines to canopy the arbor. It was a promise of grape rewards.

~◊~

Three years later . . . "Kiddo, come on out here . . . I want to show you something."

Joining Robert in the arbor, I looked up to where he was pointing.

"Do you see it?"

"See what, Hon?"

"Right there, see?" He kept pointing.

"What am I supposed to see?"

Patiently, Robert cupped my small face in his large hands and gently pointed my eyes in the right direction.

"Grapes!" I screamed. "Oh, there's another one, there, and there . . . five, six, seven. . . ." I counted seventeen beautiful bunches of exquisite green pearls.

As the fruit took on color—pink, red, maroon—the attack of the bulbuls came fast and furious. A third of the crop was lost before I protected my precious grapes with an arsenal of homemade bird deterrents that consisted of an assortment of ribbons, dangling CDs, and pinwheels.

"They have to eat, too," Robert joked, but I didn't think it was funny.

Mona smiled as she presented me with a perfect bunch of red flame grapes. "Happy 80th birthday, Mom."

I know now, why I've always wanted a grape vine. I have learned the lessons from my arbor. As I tend to my grapes—lifting, guiding, supporting, and pruning the vines— so too, has He lifted, guided, supported, and disciplined me. I am truly thankful to be blessed by the abundance in my life.

The arbor is a haven for my family and myself. As the generations that follow take over the care of the grape vines, they too, shall learn the lessons from my arbor.

Bob and Mona are carpenters in their hearts . . .

Grape Rewards

# *MY CUP RUNNETH OVER

If I had known I would live this long, I would have saved more money. . . . Truth be known, money was never a driving force, or a measure of success for me.

My first awareness of the passage of time was a rude awakening on my 50th birthday—a half-a-century—so old.

"I'm depressed," I complained to brother Jay.

"I should be so lucky," Jay said. "You've come a long way, Sis . . . here's wishing you more of the same."

From humble beginnings as a barefoot girl on the streets of Kalihi to a sophisticated globetrotter, my ordinary life has been a fantastic journey.

Each step, every turn or fork in the road, and the ups and downs of my roller coaster life has been blessed with the caring and loving presence of family, friends, and kind strangers. They were there for me at the exact time and place when I needed them—for a reason. I did not question the reason, I simply accepted.

I am comforted in my belief that I, in turn, have lifted spirits with a smile, warmed hearts with a hug, and reawakened the joys of life with a pat on the back— just being there—for those many people who crossed my path.

And so, my adventure continues . . . one day at a time.

I will enjoy my journey—the destination will come soon enough—adding to my *One Cup Rice*, one grain at a time.

Should you stop for me when I'm crossing Waialae Avenue, help me select nice papayas at the Open Market, or sit next to me to try your luck on the slots at the Fremont, I will smile. When you smile back, that moment will begin *our* adventure —however short or long—and I will add another grain to my *One Cup Rice*.

My cup runneth over. . . .

*"My cup runneth over.
Surely goodness and mercy
shall follow me all the days
of my life."*

*Psalm 23:5-6*

# EPILOGUE

Mom said, "Write." She reminded me that I was always a writer—thank you notes, diaries, journals, letters, poems, stories, newswriting, yearbooks, high school plays—and an avid reader. I would look up from a read and tell Mom, "I can write that. . . ."

~◊~

Fourth grade classmates can be cruel in their critique of a fairy tale. Eddie taunted, "Can I be your frog prince?" The other kids laughed and snickered, "You, a princess? Whoever heard of a four-eyed princess?" No matter, I kept writing, but I stopped sharing my stories with them. Instead, I shared my stories with Teddy. He always sat nicely and gave me his complete attention. His direct eye contact and ever-present smile encouraged me. Teddy never laughed or made fun of my stories. Teddy was my best friend.

~◊~

Newswriting class at Kawananakoa Intermediate School introduced me to a different kind of writing. I enjoyed interviewing classmates and teachers, and reporting school activities and events. Research satisfied my appetite for knowledge. I had dreams of becoming the *"Lois Lane"* of a Honolulu newspaper.

"Girls Need Math, Too," was one of my crusader articles, written in protest of not being approved for algebra class. I needed Mr. O's approval for this class and he questioned, "Why do you want to take algebra?"

"I need algebra, because. . . ."

"You'll get married, have some kids, and never make use of algebra. You're wasting your time and mine . . . disapproved."

I answered Mr. O.'s "why" with my "because" and protested his gender bias in my next editorial in the school newspaper. My article was "killed" by my advisor, Mrs. C., who warned me it was not politically wise.

Writing was so much a part of my life, I wrote stories in Japanese. *Tsuzuri kata* assignment from Mr. N. at Palama Gakuen Japanese Language School was always a challenge. The winner of the best story received a prize at the awards ceremony held at the end of the school year. Mom was happy about all the prizes I won—pen and pencil sets, books, magazine subscriptions, composition books, ink and brush sets. I used all of them to further my studies. Mom was most proud of the Japanese-English dictionary. She said it was worth her saving and paying the *gessha* (monthly tuition).

Study and classroom enactments of Shaw's *Pygmalion*, O'Neal's *The Hairy Ape* and Shakespeare's comedies and tragedies—the usual drama curriculum—became boring for those of us who had been taking drama class for two years. The class and the Theater Guild Club at Farrington High School voted to try something different. "The Shepherdess," my script written for the Guild was selected for production. "Hurray for Hollywood," big stars, big movies, big money . . . dream on. . . .

Meanwhile, back on planet Earth . . . working my way up from payroll clerk, clerk-stenographer, medical secretary, supervisor of a steno pool, to manager of a Word Processing Center, my job required writing of a technical nature. As challenging as it was, I'm relieved I'll never have to write another SOP (Standard Operating Procedure).

~◊~

Postcards and letters home to family about our travels kept me writing during my retirement years.

"Mom, you and dad should share your knowledge and experiences about salmon fishing. You can't take it with you." At our son Bob's coaxing, my first book, "The Salmon Fishing Adventure: How to Locate, Lure, and Land the Big Salmon and More," was published in the summer of 2004.

Where did I put those postcards, letters, and photographs? I could write more travel adventure books. Science fiction is my favorite read . . . a steamy romance set in outer space? Teddy, my best friend, can you play back the children's stories I wrote and read to you—oh, so long ago?

"Okay, Mom, okay . . . I'll write . . . I'll write. . . ."

# GLOSSARY

adobo (Filipino: Pork or chicken cooked in vinegar)
arigato (Japanese: Thank you)
aweoaweo (Hawaiian: A red fish with big eyes)
chanoyu (Japanese: Tea ceremony)
dashi (Japanese: Soup stock)
gau gee (Chinese: Deep fried pork and vegetable wrap)
geisha (Japanese: Artist of Japanese entertainment)
gessha (Japanese: Tuition)
gohan (Japanese: Cooked rice)
guisantes (Filipino: Pork, peas, red peppers in tomato
      sauce)
gyoza (Japanese: Dumpling)
hanai (Hawaiian: Adopt)
hanamichi (Japanese: Passageway that runs from the
      back of the theater to the center stage)
hapuu (Hawaiian: Tree fern)
hayaku (Japanese: Hurry, quickly)
heiwa (Japanese: Peace)
hime ningyo (Japanese: Princess doll)
Hina Matsuri (Japanese: Girls' Day Festival)
ikebana (Japanese: Flower arrangement)
ikenai (Japanese: Unacceptable)
jai (Chinese: Vegetarian dish)
juk (Chinese: Rice soup)
kago (Japanese: Hand bag)
kalbi (Korean: Barbecued ribs)
Kanikapila (Hawaiian: Festival)
kanji (Chinese characters used in Japanese writing)
kanzashi (Japanese: Hair ornament)

kim chee (Korean: Pickled vegetables)
kimono (Japanese dress)
kimpira (Japanese: Cooked burdock roots)
kome (Japanese: Raw rice)
koto (Japanese: A thirteen-string musical instrument)
kumu (Hawaiian: Goat fish)
lanai (Hawaiian: Porch)
Lapinha (Portuguese: Nativity scene)
lau lau (Hawaiian: Pork, fish and taro leaves wrapped
    in ti leaves)
lilikoi (Hawaiian: Passion fruit)
lumpia (Filipino: Meat and vegetables wrap)
luna (Hawaiian: Foreman)
maioghi (Japanese: Fan for dancing)
malassadas (Portuguese: Doughnuts)
mandoo (Korean: Beef and vegetable dumplings)
miso (Japanese: Fermented soy bean paste)
muu muu (Hawaiian: Loose dress)
Nanay (Filipino: Grandmother)
niitsuke (Japanese: Fish cooked in sugar, soy and
    ginger sauce)
nishime (Japanese: Cooked mixed vegetables)
obi (Japanese: Kimono sash)
odori (Japanese: Dance)
ojiisan (Japanese: Grandfather)
okai (Japanese: Rice soup)
okaasan (Japanese: Mother)
okesho (Japanese: Makeup)
ono (Hawaiian: Delicious)
ozashiki (Japanese: Tatami rooms for entertainment)
pikake (Hawaiian: Jasmine)
poi (Hawaiian: Cooked taro pounded into paste)
poke (Hawaiian: Cubed raw fish appetizer)

Popo (Chinese:  Grandmother)
pupu (Hawaiian: Appetizer, snack)
saiho (Japanese: Kimono sewing)
saimin (Japanese: Noodles in broth with vegetable and
    meat garnishes)
sansei (Japanese: Third generation)
sashimi (Japanese: Sliced raw fish or seafood)
shamisen (Japanese: Three-stringed instrument played
    with a plectrum)
Shogatsu (Japanese:  New Year)
Showa ninen (Japanese: Second year of the Showa
    era)
somen (Japanese: Noodles)
sushi (Japanese: Raw seafood slices on rice)
tabi (Japanese: Socks)
tako (Japanese: Octopus)
tansu (Japanese: Chest of drawers)
tatami (Japanese: Straw floor mat)
tempura (Japanese: Deep fried shrimp and vegetables)
Tinikling (Filipino: Bamboo dance)
Tutu (Hawaiian:  Grandmother)
wi "vee" (Hawaiian:  A round, yellow-orange-skinned fruit
    with fibrous pulp)
yurei (Japanese:  Ghost)